Healing Presence

Stories of Faith and Hope

Kathy —
may you always know
God's Healing Presence —
Joanna
8/07

Rev. Joanna J. Seibert, M. D.

Deacon, Trinity Episcopal Cathedral,
Little Rock, Arkansas
Former Director of Radiology,
Arkansas Children's Hospital
Professor of Radiology and Pediatrics,
University of Arkansas for Medical Sciences

*T*emenos Publishing ~ Little Rock, AR

Cover art by Mitchell Crisp Patterson
Cover photo by Emily Bost
(The artist who created the statue was a student at William Carey College. Records of his name were lost in Hurricane Katrina in 2005 when it devastated the Mississippi Gulf Coast.)

A portion of the proceeds from the sale of *Healing Presence* will go to St. Peter's by the Sea in Gulfport, Mississippi

ISBN 0-9785648-4-7

*T*emenos Publishing
303 Rice St.
Little Rock, AR 72205
501-920-7803
www.temenospublishing.com

To the brave friends, patients, and families who shared their stories to make this book possible.

And to my husband Robert and children John, Joanna, and Robert, and their very dear families, who have taught me the meaning of presence.

Preface

Joanna Seibert has written a remarkable book. Like a classic drama, it touched me a level far below her poignantly real and moving stories. Although I learned a number of effective personal things to do to help people, I realized early on that the author was describing a unique Christian style of care-giving, in which hospital staff, friends, and everyone in a patient's family may unknowingly be potential channels of God's healing presence. When she steps into a hospital room, she sees not only the suffering of the patient and the family members. She also sees and describes with poetic clarity things much greater than the suffering. In specific loving actions of family members, hospital staff, and friends of the patient, Joanna sees the healing presence of a loving and compassionate Lord—acting through one or more people in the room. Her style is to join what is already in progress and to supplement the loving of the healing presence already at work. This cooperative partnering is no mere symbolism, but is a living sacrament of Christ's body.

One example of finding God already at work involved a dying eight year old girl Joanna knew to be in excruciating pain. Lying on the child's bed was a large grandmother, surrounding the dying girl with her great, gentle arms and body, relieving by her silent presence pain that could not be relieved medically. The author said, "I stood in awe, for I knew I was on holy ground. I was in the presence of the living God."

This wise physician and loving deacon-caregiver taught me many important things in HEALING PRESENCE, but none greater than how to see with new eyes that patients are not alone in their pain and fear—and that we care-givers aren't either.

Keith Miller
The Taste of New Wine
A Hunger for Healing
What to do with the Rest of Your Life
The Edge of Adventure (with Bruce Larson)

Foreword

Compassion is a much-touted Christian virtue that is also a bit of a conundrum. That is, as religions go, it is far more readily associated with—and definitely more emphasized within—Buddhism than Christianity. Certainly the western polities that have risen out of the Christian ethos could hardly be characterized as having been abundant with compassion. The difference perhaps is that somewhere along the way, we western Christians, unlike our Buddhist brothers and sisters, lost the notion that virtues have to be honed consciously and continuously. In our affluence, the sparse life became, with each passing century, harder to desire, much less attain until, as the poet says, we forgot to remember. What Joanna Seibert does in this little manual is to force our hand.

I do not mean to imply that Seibert delivers here a treatise on the spiritual disciplines, much less on compassion per se. Nothing could be farther from the truth of the thing. All she does in these pages is just tell us stories...stories about ordinary people facing the ordinary burdens of intractable pain, terminal illness, dementia, debility, and death. Ordinary stories about the life agonies that make of us all brothers and sisters within the bonds of our common and inescapable flesh.

Seibert's are simple stories, even, ones that show rather than say the attitudes of heart and of daily decision-making that are the exercise of compassion. Clearly she thinks that each of us within the practice of our Christian faith is called to be pastor to all who chance to come with need into our ken. And for both the pastorally trained and the lay untrained, she offers the practical tools of appropriate prayers and soothing words, all very good to be aware of and have ready to hand; but those tools likewise are not the real gift of this book. The real gift is caught succinctly and precisely in its title.

Presence, Seibert teaches us, is in reality all we can give to one another. When pain has riveted the attention to itself, when fear has encapsulated the soul, when necessity lies beyond the reach of any relief—when these things come, as they do to every one of us—then only presence can surmount the barriers and enter into the suffering with the sufferer. Presence is the incarnation of compassion; and being present in the name and spirit of Jesus lies like a treasure within the center of every Christian, if only we can begin to remember not to forget.

Joanna Seibert's stories will help us in the necessary business of remembering.

Phyllis Tickle
The Farm in Lucy
Sixth Week of Pentecost, 2005

Table of Contents

God does not give answers to Job and his companions about why all these terrible disasters happen to him, but instead God sends his presence to Job. Our experience is that in any relationship, presence is more powerful than answers. We certainly do not have answers, but God calls us to bring our presence to those who, like Job, have experienced the pain and sorrow of this life.

Introduction

"He came out and went, as was his custom, to the Mount of Olives; and the disciples followed him. When he reached the place, he said to them, 'Pray that you may not come into the time of trial.' Then he withdrew from them about a stone's throw, knelt down, and prayed. 'Father, if you are willing, remove this cup from me; yet, not my will but yours be done.' Then an angel from heaven appeared to him and gave him strength. In his anguish he prayed more earnestly, and his sweat became like great drops of blood falling down on the ground. When he got up from prayer, he came to the disciples and found them sleeping because of grief, and he said to them, 'Why are you sleeping? Get up and pray that you may not come into the time of trial.'" Luke 22: 39-46.

For over 60 years I have been searching for a relationship with Jesus. I am in communion with God, the Father, and God, the Mother, and God, the Holy Spirit. Yet I seem not to be able to have that personal relationship with the historical Jesus that I hear so many of my friends talk about. I know his story, but I have not felt his personal presence until recently. I have met our Lord, not in the church's sanctuary, but in the garden of all places—the Garden of Gethsemane. I find the Garden not in the beauty of the outdoors, but in the homes of the sick, nursing homes, and hospitals. There I meet the aged, the wounded, cancer victims, the newborn, the young, men and women speechless and paralyzed by stroke, young and old disabled by heart disease. They are all in that Garden praying as Christ did that this cup will pass them by. And I am there praying with them that they may not need to drink from this cup. The picture of Christ at Gethsemane hung behind the pulpit in the small-town Methodist church in Virginia of my growing up years. I have no difficulty visualizing it. But today I see the faces of those whom I visit in the hospital in that picture. I see and hear their prayers and the prayers of their families so earnest that sometimes I wonder if blood will not soon appear in the sweat on their foreheads.

What do you say to the husband who is about to lose his wife to cancer when he tells you, "I can't lose her, she is my life"? What do you say to the young mother whose son has drowned? What do you say to the friend who is your age who has undergone every possible treatment for her cancer, but her disease is coming back with a vengeance? What do you say to the blessed man who has lived a life of serving others for over 80 years who is incontinent, can not walk, and can not remember what he had for breakfast much less your last visit? This is where I meet Christ and the suffering he endured. I do not understand why they must suffer. Some receive miraculous cures, but others don't. They must drink from a cup we all wished had passed them by. I don't understand this, either.

I do know, however, that the living Christ is there within and beside each of the sick and their loved ones. And sometimes I can see the angels he has sent to guard over them—nurses and physicians and health professionals who go an extra mile, the ones who see their work as a ministry and not just a source of income.

If you are like myself, searching for the Christ, I know a place where you can find him and I know he will dwell there until all are healed and there will no longer be any suffering and every tear wiped dry.

Prayer for People Critically Ill, or Facing Great Uncertainty

God of the present moment,
God who in Jesus stills the storm
And soothes the frantic heart;
Bring hope and courage to *N*
As *s/he/they*
Wait/s in uncertainty.
Bring hope that you will make *her /him/ them* the equal
Of whatever lies ahead.
Bring *her/ him/ them* courage to endure what cannot be avoided,
For your will is health and wholeness;
You are God, and we need you.
—*New Zealand Prayer Book*, p. 747.

I.

MEETING HIM IN THE GARDEN

John 20: 11-18

"Mary Magdalene went and announced to the disciples, "I have seen the Lord.""

"THE UNIVERSE IS MADE OF STORIES, NOT OF ATOMS."

—Muriel Rukeyser

The Grandmother

"Just as there were many who were astonished at him-—so marred was his appearance, beyond human semblance, and his form beyond that of mortals…" Isaiah 52: 14.

I still so well remember the day I visited the room of an eight-year-old girl dying of cancer at Children's Hospital. I went to perform a test to try to explain and relieve some of her suffering. Her disease and its treatment had greatly disfigured her body. Her head was almost bald with sparsely scattered streaks of once-curly blond hair. The dark sunken eyes on her ashen face were highlighted by purple blotches beneath her pale skin from previous bleeding episodes. Her paper thin skin seemed attached directly to the bones of her arms and legs. Her breathing was intermittent and labored. Each movement of her frail body took all of her energy. She was in constant pain.

As I entered her room, I was overcome immediately by her suffering—so unjust, unfair, unreasonable. This has been my closest experience of the horror of the crucifixion. But in the midst of this great suffering I also encountered something even more overpowering. This young innocent had not been abandoned. She was not alone. Lying in bed beside the almost lifeless child was her grandmother. This grandmother's huge body was embracing and surrounding this precious inhuman suffering. I stood in awe, for I knew I was on holy ground. I was in the presence of the living God.

I will never forget the great, gentle arms and body of this grandmother. She never spoke while I was there. She was holding and participating in suffering that she could not relieve, and somehow her silent presence was relieving it. No words could express the magnitude of her love. I had been there before. I knew immediately that this was what my grandmother would have done for me if I had been that child.

I performed my test as quickly as possible, but stood at the door a moment longer, the image of this little girl and her grandmother searing into my heart. In silence I turned and walked out, the door shutting gently behind me.

Prayer for a Sick Child

Lord Jesus Christ, Good Shepherd of the sheep, you gather the lambs in your arms and carry them in your bosom: We commend to your loving care this child N. Relieve *his* pain, guard *him* from all danger, restore to *him* your gifts of gladness and strength, and raise *him* up to a life of service to you. Hear us, we pray, for your dear Name's sake. Amen. —*Book of Common Prayer* (*BCP*), p. 459.

The Hands of God

"A leper came to him begging him, and kneeling he said to him, 'If you choose, you can make me clean.' Moved with pity, Jesus stretched out his hand and touched him, and said to him, 'I choose. Be made clean!' Immediately the leprosy left him, and he was made clean." Mark 1: 40-41.

Today I sit at sunset near the Sanctus candle in our historic chapel as I wait for the midweek Eucharist and healing service to begin. I remember the first time I participated in this ancient liturgy of healing with the laying of hands on our heads and the anointing of our foreheads with oil. The familiar words of healing chant in my ears, "I lay my hands upon you in the Name of our Lord and Savior Jesus Christ, beseeching him to uphold you and fill you with his grace, that you may know the healing power of his love." At that first healing service I did not want to leave the altar rail. When I slowly raised my head, I saw friends across the altar from me. As our priest and our other deacon were anointing each bowed head, other members on either side of them were putting their hands on the anointed one's shoulders and praying for her healing as well. I was moved by being in the presence of a community of believers, recognizing our defects, praying for forgiveness, asking for the grace to be changed in mind, body, and spirit, and reaching out to each other by physically praying for each other's healing. I felt I was on holy ground, a place where the human and the divine were joined together. Our humanness had been blessed and anointed by the God who not only holds each of us in his arms, but also is present in each of our neighbors' hands as well as our own.

The Sanctus candle flickers in front of me as this evening's congregation begins to file in. I am again transported back, now to an early morning healing service in the Bethlehem Chapel at the National Cathedral some years ago. That chapel is especially beautiful in the quiet of the early dawn. We literally heard angel voices as the new Cathedral choir for girls was practicing above us for their first Evensong. From my back row seat, I watched people come in to begin their new day with new life. Some were in sandals; some wore high heels and business suits. Some hurried late; others had been there praying when I arrived. As others knelt for the laying on of hands and the anointing of oil at the altar, I became acutely aware that there was more pain in the world than my own. I felt connected to the pain and suffering of my brothers and sisters at that place. Then as the priest laid his hands upon my head, I felt the warmth of many other hands on my back. Others from the congregation were also laying their hands on each of us at the altar and silently praying for healing. I felt the warmth and strength of a community in a sacred space lifting me up—a community I would never know or see again. I knew I was experiencing the physical presence of "the hands of God." I still feel the warmth of those hands on my shoulders and back tonight. I silently pray that I may carry their strength and prayers with me and that I in turn may bring comfort and strength to others as that congregation did to me.

I close my eyes as this evening's liturgy begins. I am taken back to a healing service at a church called Holy Spirit on the Gulf Coast. I met the Holy Spirit there. After members knelt for healing, many in the congregation stayed at the altar to lay on hands with their priest. There again was a community praying and reaching out to one another for healing. Couples knelt together; mothers and daughters, fathers and sons, knelt beside each other. Handicapped members who could not kneel stood while others in their community held them up. Obviously ill members knelt and asked for healing for others as well as themselves. I was especially moved by a small child who asked an older woman as she left the altar, "When he laid his hand on you, did it hurt?" Children have so much more insight than we do. Yes, my experience is that healing hurts. Anyone who has had surgery or any physical injury knows well the many painful days, weeks, and months that accompany healing. It is often a very slow process as well. Life has taught me that spiritual healing is the same. I must first realize my wounded-ness and ask for healing. I must be on my knees. The physical presence of those I worship with tonight will also make healing a little more bearable. Something mystical occurs here that I cannot explain. Even my years of medical practice do not offer any hope of explanation, only more mystery.

The scripture readings and litany of healing have ended. I stand out from the prayer desk across from the Sanctus candle and walk the short distance to the altar. The cushion is soft under my knees, the rail hard under my elbows. I bow my head and allow the healing oil to wash over me like rain as our priest anoints me. Then I rise and place my hands and the oil on another's head.

Prayer for Use of Oil

God of healing and hope,
Your Son our Saviour sent his disciples
To anoint the sick with oil;
Fulfill your promise through this oil
Which we set apart in his name
To be used as a sign of forgiveness,
Healing and salvation.
—*New Zealand Prayer Book*, p. 746.

Laura's Easter Corsage

"For he will deliver you from the snare of the fowler
and from the deadly pestilence;
he will cover you with his pinions;
and under his wings you will find refuge;
his faithfulness is a shield and buckler.
You will not fear the terror of the night,
Or the arrow that flies by day."   Psalm 91: 3-5.

A child wore the last Easter corsage I remember. I still clearly see this young four-year-old patient I cared for over twenty-five years ago. Laura was small for her age and ravaged with a deadly tumor, neuroblastoma. Do I remember her so well because she was my daughter's age? I see her sunken blue eyes and the blond hair that came and went with her chemotherapy. I remember just as vividly Laura's mother, who watched her fragile daughter suffer through a long and painful death.

I particularly remember Laura's last Easter weekend. She was lying beneath a large nuclear medicine camera to monitor her recent bone metastases. Pinned to her tiny yellow robe was her Easter corsage of red roses and baby's breath. Her mother sang softly as she held her daughter's frail, pain-ridden body quiet for the study. As she almost surrounded Laura with her body, she too was covered by the imposing medical camera.

That scene will always remain my image of the God who cares for those who suffer. He takes the test with us. God surrounds us with his love, gets under the camera with us, weeps with us, gives us red roses to wear even in the midst of our suffering, and sings softly in our ear.

Prayer in Times of Personal Distress

Lord Christ, you came into the world as one of us, and suffered as we do. As we go through the trials of life, help us to realize that you are with us at all times and in all things; that we have no secrets from you; and that your loving grace enfolds us for eternity. In the security of your embrace we pray. Amen. —*Enriching Our Worship 2*, p. 69.

Magnificat

"My soul proclaims the greatness of the Lord,
My spirit rejoices in God my Savior,
For he has looked with favor on his lowly servant.
From this day all generations will call me blessed;
The Almighty has done great things for me,
And holy is his Name." Luke 1: 46-49.

A group of women at St. Margaret's regularly go to the hospital after the birth of a child from our congregation. We pray the short service in the *Book of Common Prayer* for "Thanksgiving for the Birth of a Child." It has become one of my most favorite services. All the women read the part of the celebrant. The new mother reads the Magnificat. The father reads Psalm 116. The Song of Mary now has new meaning for all of us. This is the song that Mary sang to Elizabeth as the two pregnant cousins met, and Elizabeth recognized the presence of God in her relative. As I read the passage, I not only hear the voice of Mary but I also hear the voices and see the faces and tears of so many other new mothers we have met with their newborn babies in their arms. I also hear the voice of new fathers reading how they "love the LORD, because he has heard the voice of my supplication; because he has inclined his ear to me whenever I called upon him." We only stay a very short time, for this is usually the day after delivery. It is, however, an unbelievable service of thanksgiving in a community of women for the most precious of all gifts—the gift of life formed out of

God's love.

This past year I again offered this liturgy of thanksgiving with the women of our church, but this time it was our daughter-in-law reading the Magnificat after the birth of our first grandchild. Our son read Psalm 116 while they both held our newly-born granddaughter, Langley Grace. Indeed I know what Grace is. It is a precious grandchild.

When my husband and I renewed our marriage vows at our twentieth wedding anniversary over ten years ago, this same son read Psalm 128. As I looked at Langley Grace's newborn eyes, the words again rang in my ears, "The LORD bless you from Zion. May you see the prosperity of Jerusalem all the days of your life. May you see your children's children."

The promises of these two Psalms and Mary's Song echoed through the room in the voices of the women, my family, and even Langley's cries, and it was more beautiful than I could have imagined. And I knew there was a new presence of God in our lives.

Prayer for Thanksgiving of a Birth of a Child

O God, you have taught us through your blessed Son that whoever receives a little child in the name of Christ receives Christ himself; we give you thanks for the blessing you have bestowed upon this family in giving them a child. Confirm their joy by a lively sense of you presence with them, and give them calm strength and patient wisdom as they seek to bring this child to love all that is true and noble, just and pure, lovable and gracious, excellent and admirable, following the example of our Lord and Savior, Jesus Christ. Amen. —BCP, p. 443.

II.

FRIENDS CARRYING THE PARALYTIC

MARK 2: 1-12

"Then some people came, bringing to him a paralyzed man, carried by four of them. And when they could not bring him to Jesus because of the crowd, they removed the roof above him; and after having dug through it, they let down the mat on which the paralytic lay. When Jesus saw their faith, he said to the paralytic, 'Son, your sins are forgiven.'"

"MAY THE SPIRIT BLESS YOU WITH DISCOMFORT AT EASY ANSWERS, HALF-TRUTHS AND SUPERFICIAL RELATIONSHIPS SO THAT YOU WILL LIVE DEEP IN YOUR HEART. AND MAY THE SPIRIT BLESS YOU WITH THE FOOLISHNESS TO THINK YOU CAN MAKE A DIFFERENCE IN THE WORLD, SO THAT YOU WILL DO THE THINGS WHICH OTHERS SAY CANNOT BE DONE."

—Interfaith Council for Peace and Justice, Ann Arbor, Michigan

Prayer Group

"Are any among you suffering? They should pray. Are any cheerful? They should sing songs of praise. Are any among you sick? They should call for the elders of the church and have them pray over them, anointing them with oil in the name of the Lord. The prayer of faith will save the sick, and the Lord will raise them up; and anyone who has committed sins will be forgiven. Therefore confess your sins to one another, and pray for one another, so that you may be healed. The prayer of the righteous is powerful and effective." James 5: 13-16.

We met every Saturday at 1:00 p.m. at their home for prayers. It had been our vicar's suggestion. Charles had been diagnosed with advanced esophageal cancer. How could we respond? He had been active as an usher. Nancy had been an anchor member of our card team, sending notes to first time visitors, lapsed and returning members.

Members of the card and usher teams now met with them every week. We did African Bible study using scripture from the healing service. One member read the scripture; we each shared the word or phrase that caught our attention; someone reread the passage; we shared how the passage touched our life; we read the passage again; we shared how God might want to change us; and then we prayed for each other. We sometimes had a healing service. We laughed, we cried, we prayed.

The group kept meeting after he died. We had become family.

Prayer at Healing Service

Almighty and eternal God, so draw our hearts to you, so guide our minds, so fill our imaginations, so control our wills, that we may be wholly yours, utterly dedicated to you; and then use us, we pray as you will, and always to your glory and the welfare of your people; through our Lord and Savior Jesus Christ. Amen. —*The Book of Occasional Services*, p. 171.

Charles

Church of Christ

"As a deer longs for flowing streams,
So my soul longs for you, O God.
My soul thirsts for God,
For the living God." Psalm 42: 1-2.

He is 91 years old, the grandfather of a member of our parish. He has fallen and has sustained a blood clot on the brain and is just recovering from his surgery. I meet this wiry, thin gentleman for the first time in surgical intensive care as his favorite nurse is feeding him. He can eat only very soft foods, for he has only a few remaining teeth in place.

We talk about his granddaughter, his great grandchildren, and money, and mostly about how he hates being in a nursing home but yet he misses those familiar surroundings and longs to be back there. He then tells me he is "Church of Christ." He knows I am an Episcopalian. He tells me that those who think their religion is "the one" are greatly in error. Am I listening to a prophet?

I ask if we can say prayers. We pray the Lord's Prayer. Tears fill his eyes and he can barely speak. I see that longing in his eyes for spiritual food. This is not the first time I have seen this. With few exceptions, all those I visit long to say prayers and make connection to a power greater than themselves. Yet, so often we are reluctant to offer prayers to those we visit.

As his voice cracks, I feel barriers between the two of us and barriers between each of us and God crack and crumble right in front of us as well. Together we have walked through a door that has always been open but has so often been obscured by the differences in the doctrines of our faith groups. My church does not have all the answers; his "Church of Christ" does not have all the answers. But somehow our prayers together, praying a prayer that is part of both of our traditions, is a pathway to and through that door to the living Christ.

I stay and pray with him until he falls asleep, and then I continue praying for both of us in sync with his calm, rhythmic breaths.

For the Aged

Look, with mercy, O God our Father, on all whose increasing years bring them weakness, distress, or isolation. Provide for them homes of dignity and peace; give them understanding helpers, and the willingness to accept help; and, as their strength diminishes, increase their faith, and their assurance of your love. This we ask in the name of Jesus Christ our Lord. Amen. —*BCP*, p. 830.

The Lost Talent

"Or what woman having ten silver coins, if she loses one of them, does not light a lamp, sweep the house, and search carefully until she finds it? When she has found it, she calls together her friends and neighbors, saying 'Rejoice with me, for I have found the coin that I had lost.'" Luke 15: 8-9.

She called to ask for a visit and prayers. Her prayers were for the return of her voice, which had become swollen and transformed, as had her body by the massive dose of steroids she had been receiving for her autoimmune disease. She had been an opera singer. She had coached one of our children when he had an interest in the opera. I had stood beside her in choirs and followed her lead. She had lost her major talent and sense of ministry. As I listened to her raspy, struggling voice, I thought of other talented and gifted ones whom I had visited who also lost what they most prized that had been their sense of identity.

Mary Margaret was a renowned speech teacher who shared our pew at church many years ago (or more properly, we shared her pew). After her retirement, she suffered a devastating stroke. Her meticulous speech had become often not understandable, but her will to recover was like none I have ever seen. When we first visited, it was evening and we said Compline together. Her words were like another language, but when we came to the Lord's Prayer, she was even more determined. I could understand her first words—Our Father. Several weeks later on our next visit, almost as soon as we embraced she brought out a card for an abbreviated service she had been saying with our priest on his visits—and she pointed to the Lord's Prayer. We said it together and already so many more words were recognizable. Tears flowed from both of us. God spoke so clearly through her and her heavenly language. I can no longer say this prayer without hearing Mary Margaret.

Another friend I had visited in a nursing home had lost most of his physical and material possessions. Yet, Mr. Carter had survived years of poor health with still a rare sense of joy. Like the opera singer and Mary Margaret, his speech too was changed, this time by surgery for throat cancer. I can still hear his carbonated burp-like sounds as he sang the doxology without restrain when he was able to attend services. He, too, was a role model of determination to live fully despite tragedy and loss of loved ones and physical well being. When I visited, he would always greet me with a holy kiss and a look of love. His voice was distorted, his hair and clothes unkempt, but his eyes emitted a brightness that could illuminate a room. He introduced me as his girlfriend. He showed me the latest travel books piled by his bedside, which he had been reading. We said evening prayers—actually I said evening prayers. But when we came to the Lord's Prayer his beautiful guttural, earthy speech boomed above my softness. There was God, suffering and loving and giving praise in that nursing home. Each time I left him, I was always moved to ask Mr. Carter to pray for me. I knew I had visited a Holy Place and had been in the presence of the living God. When he died, Mr. Carter gave what remained of his body to our medical school for students to learn how to care for others.

As I quietly listened to the opera singer struggle to ask for prayers for the return of her voice, I thought of how she and the others have touched me and others in ways they would probably never know, and that God is still with us and surrounds us and loves and uses us to minister to others even when we think we have lost what once was our greatest treasure or our identity as a person. Our true identity is loving and praising and serving God, and we do not require any special talent to do this. God calls us to honor the holy in ourselves and to recognize and honor the holy in our neighbor.

I waited for her to finish talking and then I quietly replied that I would visit soon, knowing that we would pray not only for the return of her voice but for healing for both of us. And, as before, I knew I must follow her lead.

Prayer for Those Who Fear Losing Hope

Loving God, inspire by your Holy Spirit those who are afraid of losing hope, especially *N*, for whom we now pray. Give *her/him* a fresh vision of your love, that *she/he* may find again what *she/he* fears *she/he* has lost. Grant *her/him* your powerful deliverance; through the One who makes all things new, Jesus Christ our Redeemer. Amen. —*Enriching Our Worship 2*, p. 69.

Three Nursing Home Visits

"'Lord, when was it that we saw you hungry and gave you food, or thirsty and gave you something to drink? And when was it that we saw you a stranger and welcomed you, or naked and gave you clothing? And when was it that we saw you sick or in prison, and visited you?' Then the king will answer them, 'Truly I tell you, just as you did it to one of the least of these who are members of my family, you did it to me.'" Matthew 25: 37-40.

The Circle

I went into his room not knowing what to say or do. We were alone. He did not seem to recognize my presence and did not speak. I turned to the Psalms, placed his hand on the Bible, and I began reading. Soon his family came in and joined us. We circled around his bed, all held hands, and prayed. There were a few moments during the Lord's Prayer when he seemed to be with us.

The Visitor

I did not know her, but came as a group from our church to visit the nursing home. I knocked on the door. "Come in," she said. She seemed so excited to see me. Just as I sat down, her phone rang. It was her only daughter calling to check up on her. I heard her say to her daughter, "I can't talk to you now, I have a visitor." Her daughter wanted to know who it was. She answered, "I'm sorry, I am busy now with my visitor.

Call back later." We talked for some time and said prayers.

The Chance

Her daughter was out of town and asked me to visit her mother in the nursing home on Mother's Day. I went after church and was really pretty tired after preaching at three services. I took flowers from our altar. I entered her room and saw her uncomfortably hunched in her bed with her untouched dinner tray beside her. She was having difficulty feeding herself today and was depressed. "Can I help serve you your dinner?" I asked. Suddenly her whole complexion changed. I fed her the meat and mashed potatoes and cake and she told me the same stories I had heard so many times. As I sat there I was strangely warmed and energized. I thought of my mother who had died the year before. I still ached over not being able to be with her during her final days in the hospital. I realized that God was giving me one more chance to feed and care for my own mother on that special Mother's Day.

Prayer for People with Disease for Which There Is No Cure

Loving God, your heart overflows with compassion for your whole creation. Pour out your Spirit on all persons living with illness for which we have no cure, as well as their families and loved ones. Help them to know that you claim them as your own, deliver them from fear and pain, and send your archangel Raphael to minister to their needs; for the sake of Jesus Christ, our Savior. Amen. —*Enriching Our Worship 2*, p. 65.

Early Morning

"I waited patiently for the Lord; he inclined to me and heard my cry. He drew me up from the desolate pit, out of the miry bog, and set my feet upon a rock, making my steps secure. He put a new song in my mouth, a song of praise to our God. Many will see and fear, and put their trust in the Lord. Happy are those who make the Lord their trust." Psalm 40: 1-4a.

I had not planned to go to the hospital that early morning, but I had left work in a hurry the night before and had forgotten to pick up my prescriptions from the hospital pharmacy. While I was there, I decided to visit the child of some dear friends who had just been diagnosed with leukemia.

I knocked and then peeked into the darkened room. I was immediately welcomed with a massive hug and tears from the father who was there alone on a makeshift bed watching his young son sleep. I have never felt so welcomed.

"The early morning hours are the hardest," Bob said, "when everything is quiet and I have time to think."

I listened; we cried. Our prayers were interrupted by a gentle knock on the door. Ian's nurse had come to give him the medicine that would make him well.

The effects of his chemotherapy made each swallow painfully difficult. I watched as this gentle father coaxed his beloved child through this seemingly easy but very difficult procedure of just swallowing the liquid that would bring about his healing.

As the morning light peaked through the blinds, I suddenly noticed a spectacular Christmas tree in the corner of the room that had been brought in by another close friend of the family. Ian and Bob lay back down in their beds exhausted but seemingly so glad of this one more accomplishment on the road to remission and a new life.

The nurse and I left knowing that Christmas would never be the same and would always have new meaning for all of us that had come to love this family. As I drove away into the early morning traffic, I gave thanks for my forgetfulness that had led me back to this holy family.

Prayers for a Child

Gentle Jesus stay beside your child N. through this *day/night*. Take away *her/his* pain. Keep *her/him* safe. Help *her/him* in *her/his* fear. Make *her/his* body strong again and *her/his* heart glad. Thank you for your love which surrounds *her/him* always. Amen. —*Enriching Our Worship 2*, p. 64.

Ian on top of the world at Petit Jean Mountain State Park

Ian

Stealing of the Sacred

"Do not judge, and you will not be judged; do not condemn, and you will not be condemned. Forgive, and you will be forgiven; give, and it will be given to you." Luke 6: 37-38.

During a meeting at church at night, the window of my car is smashed in. I had left my communion kit, oil, and prayer book in the floor of the car in a bag that resembled a purse. As I peer through the broken glass, I see that all the sacred material I use to visit the sick is gone—stolen—taken away.

It has taking me longer than seems reasonable to work through the robbery of my visiting kit and damage to my car. I am having difficulty understanding it. My car represents my energy. The materials I use to visit the sick are sacred. A sacred part of my life has been stolen. I am depressed and have very little energy.

The next morning I go back to church to Morning Prayer. I am still grieving. On my way home I visit a member of our congregation in the hospital. She was the last person to hear the prayers that were stolen and be touched by the stolen oil blessed by our bishop. She seems better this morning. She is sitting up in bed for the first time in weeks, and there is a glow on her cheeks. Her daughter and granddaughter sit beside her, holding her hand. For that brief period that I am with her and her family, I no longer center my world on my loss and my problems. I enter into their journey and see a world larger than my own. This seems a constant about pastoral care. I go to comfort and pray for healing for someone else, and instead I am comforted and healed.

I leave her hospital room, knowing that of all things I have done to find some relief, our visit has helped the most. When I get to my car, the pain returns as I stare at the plastic covering where my window once was. I sit in my car and pray that I will soon be able no longer to carry this resentment for those who stole my sacred vessels and damaged my car, my energy. I know I will only be healed when I can forgive. Right now that may take a while. I am still in the midst of the loss and the major inconvenience imposed on my life by someone else's recklessness.

Sometimes healing takes such a long time. I pray to be open to healing and not resist it. Sometimes I seem to treasure my resentments rather than letting go. They become a well-known part of my life, like a comfortable old bathrobe.

As I start the car, I suddenly see a connection between physical and spiritual healing. I see how long it takes for physical healing in some of those I visit, while others recover miraculously. What is the secret? One secret may be that those in good physical condition do so much better. I am reminded that this may be true of spiritual healing as well. When I am having difficulty recovering from a spiritual wound, it may be that my spiritual condition was living on the edge to begin with. I was looking good on the outside, but in near critical condition on the inside. A minor incident has tipped me over the edge.

I pull away from the hospital, the morning sun warm and bright. The wind rustles the plastic on my window as I pull out into traffic and merge with the others going my direction.

Prayer at Compline

Keep watch, dear Lord, with those who work, or watch, or weep this night, and give your angels charge over those who sleep. Tend the sick, Lord Christ; give rest to the weary, bless the dying, soothe the suffering, pity the afflicted, shield the joyous; and all for your love's sake. Amen. —*BCP*, p. 134.

The Father in Law

"My child, help your father in his old age,
And do not grieve him as long as he lives;
Even if his mind fails, be patient with him;
Because you have all of your faculties, do not despise him.
For kindness to a father will not be forgotten,
And will be credited to you against your sins;
In the day of your distress, it will be remembered in your favor;
Like frost in fair weather, your sins will melt away."
Ecclesiasticus 3: 12-15.

My husband's mother died several years ago of Alzheimer's disease. Her caretaker, his father, has moved from his home of fifty years to our city and lives less than a mile from us. He is now rapidly losing his recent memory and has become very dependent on us for any joy in his life.

His life revolves around what we can do for him. He has no life of his own. He has no hobbies or other interests, except his church, which he gave up to come and live near us. He continually asks for more of our time even after we have given all that we think we can. Our feeble attempts at helping him find an independent life have failed. We cannot get him to change. We sometimes feel resentment for the demands he places on us, even though he has spent all of his life caring for others and us. We are learning how much we can do, to do it, and then set some boundaries. How very difficult to do so and not feel guilty, especially when we are dealing with one of life's kindest people.

These verses from Ecclesiasticus have brought me much comfort and have helped me find acceptance of this struggle. I have so many sins that I have not been able to make amends for to others. Perhaps any extra kindness to Bob may be motivated by other unrelated sins that still haunt me. Our behavior is so strange. I often find myself doing something extra for someone because I am trying to compensate for something wrong I have done to someone else. Often we do this without ever being aware. I pray that God will forgive my motivation for kindness and perhaps give me a few extra points for being conscious.

My experience has been that much of my walk on this journey has been an attempt to come to consciousness. It is the unconscious acts that have gotten me most into big trouble. God calls us to consciousness, and then my experience has been that he gradually heals us as we become more aware. Sometimes the healing is so very slow.

My prayer is that I will be given the grace to make an extra effort for kindness to someone whose need I will never be able to meet. May I know that this extra effort may be a means of amends for other sins for which I still seek forgiveness. May I also bring to consciousness some knowledge of exactly what I am doing. May I have strength to do what I can and have knowledge to know when I can do no more and not feel guilty for stopping.

Bob
(Photo by Andrew Kilgore)

Three Years Later

Bob is now in his late eighties. He is unable to walk since breaking both hips, has much greater dementia, and has been in a nursing home for the last three years. I still visit him for many mixed reasons. I feel a sense of duty. I love him. I want to let him know how much I appreciate all the times he so unselfishly cared for our family and me for so many years.

I am renewed when I see the smile on his face when he sees me coming. I also go because I know that God is there living at that nursing home. I see God in the Mexican aid who calls him "Papa" and treats him with the kindness and respect she would her own Papa. I see God in Jo, the African American activity director, who every day comes into that most depressing place with spirits higher than the clouds. I see God in the woman sitting beside my father-in-law in another wheelchair who stares at her surroundings and does not speak but intermittently reaches over and pats Bob's hand.

I think I have gotten over the guilt of not being able to care for him at home. Our oldest son came home for six months to care for Bob when he first developed cancer, but after he fell and broke his hip, home care became impossible for us.

I do not understand why such a wonderful and kind man has had to endure his last days with such discomfort. Bob has lived a life of thoughtfulness and caring for others. He still never complains and rarely asks for anything. I have stopped trying to understand his condition. It is similar to seeing so many children suffering with terminal diseases. But as Rabbi Kushner tells us in *When Bad Things Happen to Good People,* I can only survive this situation by concentrating on what to do next rather than spending my energy on trying to discern why this is all happening.

Bob also continues to amaze me. Recently I told him I was going to Washington, and I asked him what I should tell the president.

He thought for a while and then said, "Tell him there is an innocent man imprisoned here in Arkansas."

I said, "Oh, who is it?"

He replied, "I am that man."

Even though he cannot remember what he just had for lunch, he sometimes comes up with amazing knowledge.

Recently at a family dinner we were telling riddles that came in English Christmas crackers. Someone's riddle was, "What is the difference between 'here' and 'there?'" Before anyone else could answer, Bob spoke up: "T." I am still working on that answer myself. There is so much hidden and locked in that mind and body that unexpectedly bubbles out if we just look for it.

Bob will forget my visit by the time I reach the door of the nursing home, and yet I am magnetically drawn back to his room. Daily I long to know God. More and more I realize that our Creator is most vividly manifested in the love in Bob's face when I enter his room. He lives totally in the present. His eyes are still bright, his smile radiant. It is like seeing the veiled face of Moses or what I imagine the face of Christ must have been at the transfiguration. I know I am on holy ground. I know that in these past three years God is transforming me as he has allowed me to see him face to face.

I can no longer stay away.

Prayer for Use by a Sick Person in the Morning

This is another day, O Lord. I know not what it will bring forth, but make me ready, Lord, for whatever it may be. If I am to stand up, help me to stand bravely. If I am to sit still, help me to sit quietly. If I am to lie low, help me to do it patiently. And if I am to do nothing, let me do it gallantly. Make these words more than words, and give me the Spirit of Jesus. Amen. —*BCP*, p. 461.

Bob

Gratitude

"'Therefore I tell you,' Jesus said, 'do not worry about your life, what you will eat or what you will drink, or…what you will wear. Is not life more than food, and the body more than clothing? Look at the birds of the air; they neither sow nor reap nor gather into barns, and yet your heavenly Father feeds them. Consider the lilies of the field, how they grow; they neither toil nor spin, yet I tell you, even Solomon in all his glory was not clothed like one of these. Indeed your heavenly Father knows that you need all these things…so do not worry about tomorrow.'" Matthew 6: 25-26a, 28b-29, 32b-34a.

Almost immediately after she opened the door and invited me in, she started talking about how she recently had been diagnosed with Alzheimer's. She had decided to move into the nursing home and give up her car before life became more difficult. There was no "poor me," only "this is the reality and I am sticking to it."

She kept talking about how pleased she was, how wonderful the home was and how delightful the food was. I could hardly realize that anything was not quite right until she mentioned that she had not seen her children recently. I knew they had just been by to see her a few days before, for they had asked me to look in on her as well. I asked her about having someone pick her up to go to our church, but it was obvious that she wanted to be back in the second row pew at her own church.

I asked her if we could say prayers. She was delighted. I will never forget that powerful moment when she said, "Now, I say my prayers on my knees, but you don't have to." We both then knelt at the side of her bed. She was teaching me how to pray.

"What shall we pray for?" I asked.

She responded, "Well, every day I only pray for God's will in my life. That is the only prayer I know."

So we prayed for God's will in both our lives.

As I walked out, she said, "Your visit has given me goose-bumps."

My response was, "Perhaps you have seen mine as well."

Prayer in Loss of Memory

Holy God, you have known me from my mother's womb, and have been with me throughout my life. Protect me and keep me safe through all the changes that may come. Since I am sealed as Christ's own, help me to trust that who I am will never be lost to you. Amen. —*Enriching Our Worship 2*, p. 77.

Wounded Healer

"I said, 'I will keep watch upon my ways, so that I do not offend with my tongue. I will put a muzzle on my mouth...' So I held my tongue and said nothing; I refrained from rash words; but my pain became unbearable." Psalm 39: 1-3.

She was the most difficult person I ever visited. I dreaded each time I stood in front of her hospital door. She seemed to punch every one of my character defect buttons. She was the culmination of everyone with whom I ever had difficulty interacting. Almost every word she spoke brought back some painful memory from the past.

When I went in to see her, I knew I would not have a chance of ministering to her unless I left all my baggage at that door before I entered.

As I washed my hands before visiting her, I ritually had to wash my mind as well of past memories. For these few minutes, this visit, my world was about *her*, not me. I had come to visit her. I must listen to her, pray with her. I had to be present to her and put aside my past. I was not there to talk about or process my experiences but to listen to hers.

I learned from her that I was a wounded healer. Like all of us, I had been wounded, but my ministry to this person was to listen to her wounds. The presence of my wounds hopefully made me more open to see and hear hers. I could process my own wounds later in a pastoral care group or with a spiritual friend or advisor after this visit. But for the moment, I must be there for this person. Bless her.

As I daily kept her in my prayers, God seemed to change and transform both of us. There were even days when I looked forward to seeing her, praying that in some small way my presence would let her know how much God loved her.

It became easier as I was able to see the presence of God deep within her, and I wondered what that presence was going to teach me that day.

Collect for Third Sunday in Lent

Almighty God, you know that we have no power in ourselves to help ourselves: Keep us both outwardly in our bodies and inwardly in our souls, that we may be defended from all adversities which may happen to the body, and from all evil thoughts which may assault and hurt the soul; through Jesus Christ our Lord, who lives and reigns with you and the Holy Spirit, one God, for ever and ever. Amen —BCP, p. 218.

The Storm

"One day he got into a boat with his disciples…and as they sailed he fell asleep. And a storm of wind came down on the lake, and they were filling with water, and were in danger. And they went and woke him, saying, 'Master, Master, we are perishing!' And he awoke and rebuked the wind and the raging waves; and they ceased, and there was a calm." Luke 8: 22-25.

A powerful storm is headed for a condo that has been our family vacation home for twenty years. It is the second hurricane in nine months to hit us directly. In fact we have just hurried home from a trip to the Gulf Coast trying to make repairs from the previous hurricane.

There are so many others who are losing their only home, so many others much more seriously affected by this storm, but it is hard not to concentrate on our own tragedy.

I've been home just a few hours and drive to the hospital in the early morning to visit a much-loved member of our congregation who has been in ICU. As I arrive, three fire trucks pull up. I hurry up the stairs to ICU. They are not letting anyone in ICU because of the possible fire somewhere in the hospital. One more setback.

As I am standing there impatiently waiting, a radiant young woman comes up to me whose inner and outer beauty simply bubble out of her. "You're Dr. Seibert. I'm Anne, Tess's mother."

My mind is flooded with memories of Anne as a young doctor who had to cut short her residency when she developed cancer. Then our paths crossed again when she brought her first child Tess to Children's Hospital for tests. That must have been at least fifteen years ago. I still remember the day we found Tess's unusual cancer on ultrasound. I remember how rapidly Tess had new lesions and died much too soon. Anne's sister and her father had also died from cancer. Anne then tells me she is there this morning with her mother who is dying from cancer. They are visiting her brother in the intensive care unit who is gravely ill from treatment from his cancer.

Anne tells me how she wanted to have another child after Tess died, but her doctors advised against it since that child would have a fifty-fifty chance of also having cancer. It was now apparent that their family has a very unusual cancer gene.

Anne tried to adopt after Tess's death. Barrier after barrier prevented it.

She then went to her priest and asked, "Should I give up trying to adopt a child? Will it be impossible? Should I concentrate on other things?"

Her priest told her, "You will be able to adopt a child."

Anne prayed for guidance at Tess's grave.

That day she went home and received a phone call from a lawyer she had never met. "Dr. Murphy," said the voice on the other end, "we have a little girl who will be born tomorrow. Would you like to adopt her?"

Anne's daughter, Cheyenne, is now twelve years old. Anne radiates as she tells me how both she and Cheyenne compete in triathlons and are avid outdoors enthusiasts. She has lived through so much tragedy and is still in love with life and especially her new daughter that she would never have known.

Our hurricane seems like a gentle summer storm. I hug Anne gently, meet her mother and tell them that I would like to say prayers with her brother if they think it might be appropriate.

I turn to walk back to the ICU. Immediately I almost run into a longtime friend who is a nursing supervisor at the hospital. She always seems to show up at the right time when I am visiting.

"I just wanted to come over and say hi," says Julie.

"Julie, I can't believe you are here. Do you think you can help me get into ICU to see my friend from our church and Anne's brother?"

Julie replies, "We can't get into ICU just now, but your friend is no longer in ICU and is in a step down unit. I'll take you to her."

I take a deep breath and calmly walk with Julie to the elevator. The hurricane still spins down in the Gulf, but my inner storm has passed. God is here, teaching me what is really important in life, showing me where to go this early Sunday morning.

Julie and I are silent as the elevator doors open and we step inside.

Collect Eight Sunday After the Epiphany

Most loving Father, whose will it is for us to give thanks for all things, to fear nothing but the loss of you, and to cast all our care on you who care for us: Preserve us from faithless fears and worldly anxieties, that no clouds of this mortal life may hide from us the light of that love which is immortal, and which you have manifested to us in your Son Jesus Christ our Lord; who lives and reigns with you in the unity of the Holy Spirit, one God, now and for ever. Amen. —*BCP*, p. 216.

Tess

Cheyenne

Presence

"Then God answers Job out of the whirlwind." Job 38: 1.

I go to the hospital to make rounds.

I go to see the husband of a woman whom I knew many years ago but have not seen for some time. Her husband is in ICU. He is in a coma, no response. I say prayers.

I go to see someone from another town who is having surgery. Her priest has called us to visit for him. I come too late. She is already in surgery, but I do say prayers with her mother.

I wonder if I have been helpful today.

Then in the hall I run into an old friend who works at the hospital that I have not seen for many years. I have been trying to contact him, for I have heard that his young son has died. I can only imagine his pain.

We both stop our intended rounds and stand in the corridor of a busy hospital forgetting about the rest of the world hurrying by us. His voice trembles as he talks about his son's death and his anger and doubts about God. I see his hands clench as he asks me how the loving God he so intimately knew could allow an innocent child to suffer. I know I do not have answers to his questions.

I think of Job. God does not give answers to Job and his companions about why all these terrible disasters happen to him, but instead God sends his presence to Job. Our experience is that in any relationship, presence is more powerful than answers. We certainly do not have answers, but God calls us to bring our presence to those who like Job have experienced the pain and sorrow of this life.

I went to the hospital to make rounds, say words, and am reminded one more time that presence is the best I have to offer.

A Prayer Attributed to St. Francis

Lord, make us instruments of your peace. Where there is hatred, let us sow love; where there is injury, pardon; where there is discord, union; where there is doubt, faith; where there is despair, hope; where there is darkness, light; where there is sadness, joy. Grant that we may not so much seek to be consoled as to console; to be understood as to understand; to be loved as to love. For it is in giving that we receive; it is in pardoning that we are pardoned; and it is in dying that we are born to eternal life. Amen. —BCP, p. 833.

The Lord's Prayer

"Hear my prayer, O God;
give ear to the words of my mouth." Psalm 54: 2.

He was a good friend, and he was dying of cancer. He was one of the first people I ever visited pastorally. I would regularly go by in the early morning on my way to work. I so much wanted to be with him but did not know the words to say.

One morning as I was leaving, I finally timidly asked him, "Shall we pray?" I sensed instantly that we both desperately wanted to pray but did not know how to start. We sat in silence, and then he began the Lord's Prayer. From then on, each visit was the same.

We ended by holding hands and praying the Lord's Prayer. We said no other words or other prayers. I went to touch his hand, and instead I was touched by the hand of God within him.

Now several years later I still think of Bill or maybe I even feel his presence each time I pray our Lord's Prayer. They are the words to say when it is too painful to say anything else.

I think it is our Lord's Prayer, and he is praying it for us and with us.

Lord's Prayer

Our Father, who art in heaven, hallowed be thy name, thy kingdom come, thy will be done, on earth as it is in heaven. Give us this day our daily bread. And forgive us our trespasses, as we forgive those who trespass against us. And lead us not into temptation, but deliver us from evil. For thine is the kingdom, and the power, and the glory, for ever and ever. Amen. —*BCP*, p. 364.

The Anointing

"He called the twelve and began to send them out two by two, and gave them authority over the unclean spirits. So they sent out and proclaimed that all should repent. They cast out many demons, and anointed with oil many who were sick and cured them." Mark 6: 7, 12-13.

She called to say that her biopsy was negative. All of her physicians had been so certain it would be cancer. We had anointed her with oil only yesterday just before her surgery. We prayed through the tears for healing, and now it had come.

It was a miracle. She had been given new life.

We were all so excited we could barely talk. As I sat outside in the afternoon sun, I began to think of others we had recently anointed with oil and laid hands on. They were all getting better, some as expected, but some very unexpected. I was filled with a deep fear that we may have been given the power of healing.

Isn't this so human. We begin to think of our own powers and forget about the one who really uses us as a vessel to hold the oil of his healing.

Prayer at a Public Service of Healing

We lay our hands upon you and anoint you with oil in the Name of our

Lord and Savior Jesus Christ, beseeching him to uphold you and fill you with grace, that you may know the healing power of his love. Amen. —*The Book of Occasional Services*, p. 170.

III.

THE RAISING OF JAIRUS' DAUGHTER

MARK 5: 21-43

"Then one of the leaders of the synagogue named Jairus came and fell
at his feet and begged him repeatedly, 'My little daughter is at the point
of death. Come and lay your hands on her, so that she may be made
well, and live....' While he was speaking, some people came from the
leader's house to say, 'Your daughter is dead....' Jesus said to the leader
of the synagogue, 'Do not fear, only believe.'"

"DEATH IS NOT EXTINGUISHING THE LIGHT. IT IS PUTTING OUT THE LAMP BECAUSE THE DAWN HAS COME."

—Rabindrananth Tagore of India

Prayer for Kay

"This is my commandment, that you love one another as I have loved you. No one has greater love than this." John 15: 12-13a.

He knew he was dying. The third volume of Robert Caro's biography of Lyndon Johnson, *Master of the Senate*, lay between his hands. Tears welled up from his pale countenance as I walked to the bedside while Kay, his wife, was on the phone.

I asked what prayers we should say.

"I want to pray for Kay. I want to pray for our marriage."

He knew exactly the page in the prayer book. It was the prayer for the blessing of a marriage. Tears welled up and overflowed in all three of us as we heard the words: "We thank you, also, for consecrating the union of man and woman in his Name. Bless them in their work and in their companionship; in their sleeping and in their waking, in their joys and in their sorrows; in their life and in their death. Finally, in your mercy bring them to that table where your saints feast forever in your heavenly home."

As I watched his hand touch Kay's, I was suddenly reminded of the members of the ill-fated flights exactly two years before on September 11 who called home to let their loved ones know how much they cared for them just before they died: prayers for another while they were approaching death. Prayers not for themselves, but for others and their relationship with others.

The words of the blessing of their marriage hung in the hospital room like a mist, and I knew he would be praying for Kay throughout all eternity. Was this not also Christ's example for all of us to follow when he was on the cross?

I left knowing that the three of us had some glimpse of heavenly home.

The Blessing of the Marriage

Most gracious, God, we give you thanks for your tender love in sending Jesus Christ to come among us, to be born of a human mother, and to make the way of the cross to be the way of life. We thank you, also for consecrating the union of man and woman in his Name. By the power of your Holy Spirit, pour out the abundance of your blessing upon this man and this woman. Defend them from every enemy. Lead them into all peace. Let their love for each other be a seal upon their hearts, a mantle about their shoulders, and a crown upon their foreheads. Bless them in their work and in their companionship; in their sleeping and in their waking; in their joys and in their sorrows; in their life and in their death. Finally, in your mercy, bring them to that table where your saints feast for ever in your heavenly home; through Jesus Christ our Lord, who with you and the Holy Spirit lives and reigns, one God, for ever and ever. Amen. —BCP, p. 430.

Kay and Richard at Their Engagement Party

The Great Teacher

"And a woman in the city, who was a sinner… brought an alabaster jar of ointment…and began to bathe his feet with her tears and to dry them with her hair. Then she continued kissing his feet and anointing them with the ointment. …." Luke 7: 36-50.

We read the liturgy of Ash Wednesday on the first Monday of Lent, for Richard had been too ill on Ash Wednesday. Like a typical Anglican, I had my prayer book with me but did not bring the Bible. When we came to the gospel reading, Richard recited it for us even in the face of heavy sedation for pain. I saw a great memory.

With each visit, I would always ask what prayers we should say. He would always ask for prayers for Kay, never for himself. I saw pure selflessness.

One afternoon as we were about to share Eucharist together, another judge came in and of course Richard asked him to join us. I asked if there were special prayers we should say that day. Richard's response was, "Pray for the Courts: 'Almighty God, who sits in the throne judging right; we humbly beseech thee to bless the courts of justice and the magistrates in all this land; and give unto them the spirit of wisdom and understanding, that they may discern the truth, and impartially administer the law in the fear of thee alone; through his Son our Savior Jesus Christ. Amen.'"* I saw compassion.

He would often ask for special collects, the Collect of the Day, and the Psalms. I especially remember the collect for first Sunday in Lent, Psalm 42, Psalm 43, and Psalm 51. He knew them from memory. I had to use the prayer book. He tried to teach me the Latin names of the Psalms. With Richard and Kay we read together Psalm 131, *Domine, non est*, Psalm 130, *De profundis*, Psalm 139, *Domine, probasti*.

He asked if I had read Josephus. He told me how his mother had asked him to teach her Greek. She read Josephus and then they would discuss it. I knew I could not count the number of people Richard had spent hours with teaching about law, politics, the Bible, as his mother had done before him. His mother had taught seventh grade in Texarkana. She died in the classroom teaching. His brother had been in the school and had witnessed his mother's death, and his voice quivered as he spoke about how difficult that must have been for his brother. I saw true empathy.

One especially difficult day when his doctors feared he was near death, he had had many visitors. He remarked that the visitors came to talk to each other. I saw awareness and wisdom laced with humor.

We talked about the red, white and blue in all the intravenous fluids which were nourishing him, like the flag. He talked about always having a flag in his office. I commented, "And it is still here." He snappily replied, "And it should be." I saw a patriot.

We talked about his coming 68th birthday on March 26th. He was born the day after the feast day of the Annunciation of Gabriel's visit to Mary. He chuckled in his characteristic way, which I wish so much I could imitate, that his birthday was therefore too close to the annunciation for him to be the anointed one. We wondered what season he was born in. We looked up in the Prayer Book that in 1936 Easter was on April 12th. Richard almost instantly calculated that he was born on the Friday of Lent 4. His eyes glowed as he talked of the color rose being used liturgically on Lent 4 as it can be on third Sunday of Advent. He talked of a longing to see rose vestments. What extravagance to have vestments you can only wear on two Sundays of the year. He said, "It is the alabaster jar, the extravagance of the alabaster jar of ointment used by the woman who washed Jesus' feet with her tears, dried his feet with her hair, and anointed Jesus with the costly oil." I saw a life of extravagant love.

He worried that it might be a sin that sometimes his illness depressed him. Then he began to tell me how his mission in his dying was to let Kay and his family know how to live. He began to see his suffering as an awareness of the rest of the suffering in the world around him. I saw what it is like to be inclusive and related to the world.

One morning as we read Morning Prayer, he divulged one of his secrets of living. After he recited the *Te Deum*, a canticle urging us always to give thanks and praise, he told me that during these past months when doctors told him bad news about his health, he would recite the *Te Deum*, and he could make it through the difficult time.

Then he told me about a recent visit from a St. Vincent's hospital chaplain. He asked Richard did he expect a cure. "No," said Richard, "but I am hoping for management of my disease." The chaplain then said, "Let's pray for management." "No," Richard responded, "let's pray for a cure!" At that same visit he told me about plans for his funeral. He considered it a gift from him to his family and friends. He was working on his obituary as well. I saw a man living in reality but still open to a miracle.

Each visit we would also discuss whose saint day it was and was there something to learn from that saint. He constantly asked what was God teaching him in all this. He had lived with this tumor, lymphoma, for twenty-eight years. He would sometimes jokingly refer to it as "lime-oma," as it had been misspelled in one of his X-ray reports. There must be a lesson in it. Living with cancer for twenty-eight years can make you either a very grateful or very bitter person. His was a life of gratitude. "What I have learned," he said, "is to live in the present, teach Kay how to live, and now teach her how to die."

I saw a great teacher.

Te deum laudamus
You are God; we praise you;
You are the Lord; we acclaim you;
You are the eternal Father:
All creation worships you.
To you all angels, all the powers of heaven,
Cherubim and Seraphim, sing in endless praise:
    Holy, holy, holy Lord, God of power and might,
    Heaven and earth are full of you glory.
The glorious company of apostles praise you.
The noble fellowship of prophets praise you.
The white-robed army of martyrs praise you.
Throughout the world the holy Church acclaims you;
    Father, of majesty unbounded,
    your true and only Son, worthy of all worship,
    and the Holy Spirit, advocate and guide.
You, Christ, are the king of glory,
the eternal Son of the Father.
When you became man to set us free
you did not shun the Virgin's womb.
You overcame the sting of death
and opened the kingdom of heaven to all believers.
You are seated at God's right hand in glory.
We believe that you will come and be our judge.

Come then, Lord, and help your people,
bought with the price of your own blood,
and bring us with your saints
to glory everlasting.
—*BCP*, p. 95.

*BCP, p. 821.

Richard

Richard the Summer Before He Died

Sonny

"'So I say to you, Ask, and it will be given you; search, and you will find; knock, and the door will be opened for you. For everyone who asks receives, and everyone who searches finds, and for everyone who knocks, the door will be opened.'" Luke 11: 9-10.

Each time we visit he asks me, "Are you living in the moment yet?"

My answer is, "I am when I am with you."

He reminds me of how precious each day, each hour is. The past is gone; the future is an unknown. All we have is the present.

C.S. Lewis writes that living in the present is where we meet God. Sonny tells me and teaches me the same. He has survived difficult surgery with one cancer. Soon after that another cancer appears. He is given a miraculous period of remission, against all odds. But like the big bang, the clash of two cancers, takes its toll. His second cancer comes back with a vengeance.

His next question is, "What do you think about this book?"

Rarely is it one I and sometimes even his wife, Ann, have read. He tells me about little parts of it to entice me to read it. I do want to read it to gain some of his wisdom and also the author's.

I ask him what he has decided about the afterlife.

"I am finding some comfort in what Huston Smith says," as he reads with labored breath from Smith's book, *Forgotten Truth*.

Almost all of his energy is consumed in sitting up in bed. The oxygen tank and its umbilical cord are giving him the breath to continue. Yet even to the end he is still searching, searching, and sharing that search with whoever will live in the present with him.

We say prayers, confession, and share the Eucharist. Ann accuses him of taking all the wine. We laugh and say our goodbyes with a kiss.

I leave the door open behind me.

A Prayer for a Person Near Death

Almighty God, look on this your servant, lying in great weakness, and comfort *him* with the promise of life everlasting, given in the resurrection of your Son Jesus Christ our Lord. Amen. —*BCP*, p. 462.

Sonny in his Garden

The Vigil

"We do not lose heart. Even though our outer nature is wasting away, our inner nature is being renewed day by day. For this slight momentary affliction is preparing us for an eternal weight of glory beyond all measure, because we look not at what can be seen but at what cannot be seen; for what can be seen is temporary, but what cannot be seen is eternal." 2 Corinthians 4: 16-18.

The night before Jane died, we were all there. Our priest celebrated the Eucharist. Our bishop and his wife were there. I still remember seeing our bishop sitting on the floor in the hall outside of Jane's room as we took turns being with her at the vigil before her death. The bishop's chair had become the unadorned carpet of a hospital corridor.

I had heard about Jane for years. When she came to our church as Director of Christian Formation, I knew we would have a very competent woman on our staff. She was the world's greatest proponent of lay or baptismal ministry. I was in formation studying to be a deacon.

We soon clashed. She feared that my ministry as a deacon would take away from others' baptismal ministry. I feared that at every step she was blocking my diaconal ministry. We talked over tea at her house.

"Jane, I don't feel you affirm my ministry."

We talked for over an hour. She told me her fears and I told her mine. Almost instantly we became fast friends and partners.

She taught me how to be a deacon, how to lead others to their ministry. I loved working on projects with her, for she had such an eye for detail. She would pick up on so many little parts of the plan that I would miss. She had over twenty-five years of experience in Christian education.

We giggled together. We treated ourselves to shopping adventures after long days at church. We started going to Weight Watcher's together. We planned an Education for Ministry (EFM) class together.

Then her pain started. First it was vague, then more severe. She underwent multiple tests over several months. Each time a little more was revealed. Only at her exploratory surgery did they find out she had a very aggressive tumor that had been part of a disease she had had since childhood. Could I have helped her more if I had realized her childhood disease? I was flooded by so many thoughts about how I could have been a better friend.

She spent her last weeks in the hospital. I visited often, but not as much as Carol, a friend she had had for thirty years. In my prayers each night I still pray that I can be the kind of friend to someone I love as Carol was. Carol was there every day. She stayed most of the day, giving Jane's husband a much-needed respite. It wasn't just one of those in-and-out visits. I loved to hear Carol and Jane talk about their lives together, their children, their previous husbands who had died and how they comforted each other during those times, and their present husbands whom they adored and who loved them just as much.

One day Carol came in with color, for she was seeing Jane's gray hairs, and they could not have any of that.

The night of the vigil at Jane's last Eucharist, she told each of us what she wanted us to do for our ministry. I wanted to tell her, "Jane, you really should have been a deacon." She wanted me to continue to visit the sick. She wanted my husband to consider teaching the Catechesis of the Good Shepherd. That was her last homily.

I stayed until two in the morning playing the harp until she fell asleep. A nurse came in, trying to do her job of getting a blood sample to monitor the blood Jane was receiving. We asked her not to disturb Jane. I still remember the huffiness in her voice when she stomped out of the hushed room. In my prayers I hope I will remember to be more sensitive to patients instead of just concentrating on getting my job done. I saw myself in that nurse that night and prayed for both of us. I left in the wee hours. Jane's husband walked me to the car in the early morning of St. Lucy's Day.

When I got to work at the hospital at eight the next morning, my husband was at the hospital with Jane. I heard the cries of her daughter over the phone as Jane breathed her last at 8:27am. I longed to be with her. I grieved as our work at the hospital became too overwhelming for me to leave. It was not until that night after work that I could visit her family again.

At Jane's funeral, I had the privilege of playing the same harp music I had played in her hospital room that last night at her vigil. When it was time to carry her ashes to the columbarium, I had the honor of holding her veiled urn gently yet securely as we walked down the wooded path.

Jane's last picture now sits on my desk. I think of her almost daily: when laughing with a child, praying with someone in a hospital room, sitting quietly with a grieving family, teaching a class. I missed her most on Wednesday mornings when the EFM class we had planned together met without her. I knew each week that she could have led the theological reflection much better than I.

Today I feel her presence, especially in this book. In these pages is Jane's bliss, showing people how theology works in their everyday lives. This is her legacy to me that she still empowers me to share with you.

A Commendatory Prayer at the Time of Death

Into your hands, O merciful Savior, we commend you servant *N.* acknowledge, we humbly beseech you, a sheep of your own fold, a lamb of your own flock, a sinner of your own redeeming. Receive *him* into the arms of your mercy, into the blessed rest of everlasting peace, and into the glorious company of the saints in light. Amen. —*BCP*, p. 465.

Jane

Song of Simeon

"Lord, you now have set your servant free
      to go in peace as you have promised;
For these eyes of mine have seen the Savior,
      whom you have prepared for all the world to see:
A Light to enlighten the nations,
      and the glory of your people Israel." Luke 2: 29-32.

My husband's father died early this morning at one am. I stayed with him until almost nine last night. I had so much to do—work, meetings, and choir practice—all good things to do. There were weeks when I was pulled by some unknown force to visit Bob, and there were weeks when I could only be there for a short visit. But a week ago my spiritual director had told me his experience had been to listen to that inner voice that will tell me to call or visit someone. I heard that inner voice last night. That voice told me to be with Bob, and I went and spent more hours at a time with him than I had spent since his illness. By some miracle I was able to obey.

His eyes were still bright, but he was breathing rapidly because of his pneumonia. He was not febrile and said he felt no pain. We sat and held hands for several hours. I told him what a good father he had been to his family. I kissed his hand. He tried to kiss mine. He could no longer drink. We moistened his lips with water on our fingers. Our older son was with me and held his other hand. I hope I will never forget the look of joy I saw on Bob's face as he looked at his grandson for most of the night. Here was a man dying but still expressing love and joy and sending blessings to his grandson in his eyes and in his smile. I wish he could have spoken. I wondered if he was seeing his own life go by, for his grandson looks so much like him when he was that age. I kept seeing images of the veiled face of Moses, or of our Lord on the cross dying, or was it our Lord at the transfiguration? I do not know, but I know there was a burning bush near by.

I stayed until he fell asleep and was breathing easily. I thought he would live through the night. Otherwise, I would not have left him. I did not want him to die alone. There were still things I had wanted to do for him. I had planned to bring my harp and play for him today. After his wife Elizabeth had died over ten years earlier, I prayed that she would be a guardian angel to care for our children while we were apart from them. In turn, I promised her I would care for her husband. I think that Elizabeth did a better job of keeping her end of the bargain.

My husband and I and our two sons returned later that night after we received the call that Bob had died. We cried, we said prayers; we helped the nurses wash his aged body. There were roses from our church altar in his room. We put rose petals on his body and helped lift his body onto the stretcher to go to the funeral home. We walked his body out of the nursing home. We knew we were still on holy ground.

And, though I know we did all we could, it still doesn't feel like enough.

We never can do enough.

Prayers for a Vigil

Receive, O Lord, your servant, for *he* returns to you.

Wash *him* in the holy font of everlasting life, and clothe *him* in *his* heavenly wedding garment.

May *he* hear your words of invitation, "Come you blessed of my Father."

May *he* gaze upon you, Lord, face to face, and taste the blessedness of perfect rest.

May angels surround *him*, and saints welcome *him* in peace.

Into your hands, O Lord, we commend our *brother*. Amen.

—*BCP*, p. 465.

Sacred Roses

"Mary took a pound of costly perfume made of pure nard, anointed Jesus' feet, and wiped them with her hair. The house was filled with the fragrance of the perfume." John 12: 3.

I did not attend the wedding of a parishioner's daughter on Saturday night, but I knew it had to have been elegant. I imagined the church lit by the simple but stylish candelabras that were still in place before the early morning Sunday Eucharist. The flowers were spectacular with several arrangements of fall foliage mixed with red roses. They adorned our altar for both Sunday services of the Eucharist as well as an Evensong sung that night to honor St. Margaret, the patron saint of our congregation.

The next morning the Care team of our church took the flowers to the sick in nursing homes. Several of us took some of the roses to a long time friend who had been in a nursing home for almost four years.

We knew we had to take her red roses, for she had grown them in her backyard for as long as we had known her. She was very ill with pneumonia, but she would look up at the roses, and smell them, and seemed pleased. She wanted to know where we had gotten them. We told her they were from her garden. Members of her family would sometimes come in touch her face with the soft red petals after she had smelled the fragrance.

Two nights later she died with the roses still at her bedside. When family and friends gathered to say prayers, shortly after she died, we took some of the petals and scattered them over her body, just as we had done for my father-in-law. We washed her body, spread more rose petals over her, gently covered her, lifted her body up to the stretcher, and walked her out of the nursing home into the cool, silent night air. We hoped that the roses would be cremated with her body.

Today we visit her grave and now spread rose petals over the snow covered ground above her ashes. This fragrant red flower again becomes a reminder of the life of someone we so dearly loved. As we scatter the soft petals, I also remember that day at church shortly before she died and how our lives are interconnected. The same roses that celebrated the love of two young people one night also celebrated the end of a life of someone whose love was too dear for those who knew her to express in words.

Both nights, as well as on this wintry morning, the sacred can best be spoken in the softness and aroma of a red rose.

Prayer at Burial

Lord Jesus Christ, by your death you took away the sting of death: Grant to us your servants so to follow in faith where you have led the way, that we may at length fall asleep peacefully in you and wake up in your likeness; for your tender mercies' sake. Amen. —BCP, p. 504.

Lois

"Come to me, all you that are weary and are carrying heavy burdens, and I will give your rest. Take my yoke upon you, and learn from me; for I am gentle and humble in heart, and you will find rest for your souls. For my yoke is easy, and my burden is light." Matthew 11: 28-30.

She was eighty years old and a lifelong Southern Baptist. She grew up and lived almost her whole life in one small town in Arkansas. She was the mother of a member of our Education for Ministry (EFM) group.

She had bravely fought the fight against cancer for thirty-five years against insurmountable odds. The ugly dragon finally took its toll. At our many visits, in several hospitals, in and out of intensive care units, she never seemed bitter or resentful for the hand she had been dealt in this lifetime.

I suddenly realized the night she died how delicately she had been cared for by her loving God. The strong doctor who had taken care of her for thirty-five years came by that night to say goodbye and seemed lost and close to tears. She waited until her family was able to drive the four hour trip to get to the hospital to say goodbye. Her favorite nursing assistant was there. By chance, a hospice nurse was on duty on her floor that night. This nurse had never been there before. She knew exactly what to do and what to tell the family. I had planned a visit for the next morning, but something urged me to go that night instead.

I don't know if I helped Lois and her family that night, but it helped me to be in her presence one more time, to be an observer of this very special lady for one last moment before she died. Her husband was to be honored at a meeting the next day in her hometown, and she so much wanted to be there. Her children knew that now she would be there.

This gospel reading from Matthew was read in churches throughout the world the morning after Lois died. I cannot help but believe that the heavens were rejoicing that Sunday for those gentle and humble persons like Lois who carry heavy burdens but whose lives shine as if these burdens are light.

Compline

Be present, O merciful God, and protect us through the hours of this night, so that we who are wearied by the changes and chances of this life may rest in your eternal changelessness; through Jesus Christ our Lord. Amen. —*BCP*, p. 133.

Lois

The Connection

"When Mary came where Jesus was and saw him, she knelt at his feet and said to him. 'Lord, if you had been here, my brother would not have died.' When Jesus saw her weeping, and the Jews who came with her also weeping, he was greatly disturbed in spirit and deeply moved. He said, 'Where have you laid him?' They said to him, 'Lord, come and see.' Jesus began to weep." John 12: 32-35.

Miff's cancer came on so fast. I had planned to play the harp while she was getting her next chemotherapy. Early that morning I received a call from her oncologist's office that she was too sick for her treatment and had gone home. They did not expect her to live through the week. They were calling hospice that day.

I phoned her family to say I would come later in the afternoon to play. Pat, whose wife Jane had died in the past year, called to see if he could go with me. We braved the rush hour traffic only to find that Miff was finally sleeping and her family thought it best not to disturb her.

Standing in the entrance hall of their home, Pat and I talked with her husband Jim and her son. Pat knew much better what to say than I did. He alone knew Jim's pain. He said very little but his whole being had a healing presence. His body and his eyes said, "I am so sorry. I have experienced a little of what you are going through. Words cannot describe the pain."

Miff died shortly after noon the next day.

Weeks later as I spoke with Jim, I realized that we had not been called there for me to play the harp, but for Pat to connect with Jim, to let him know there was someone else who understood a little of the grief of losing the wife he so dearly loved.

Prayer for Those Who Mourn

Merciful God, whose Son Jesus wept at the death of Lazarus: look with compassion on all who are bound by sorrow and pain through the death of *N.*, a loved one. Comfort them, grant them the conviction that all things work together for good to those who love you, and help them to find sure trust and confidence in your resurrection power; through Jesus Christ our deliverer. Amen. —*Enriching Our Worship 2*, p. 111.

The Retired Priest

"He said, 'Go out and stand on the mountain before the LORD, for the LORD is about to pass by.' Now there was a great wind, so strong that it was splitting mountains and breaking rocks in pieces before the LORD, but the LORD was not in the wind; and after the wind an earthquake, but the LORD was not in the earthquake; and after the earthquake, a fire, but the LORD was not in the fire; and after the fire a sound of sheer silence." 1 Kings 19: 11-12.

He was a retired priest who had moved here from another state. It was rumored that he had almost become a bishop, but probably wasn't elected because of his rather outspoken opinions. When I first met and visited him five years ago in the hospital after his cancer surgery, he led me on a prayer book sword drill. He would tell me the prayers he wanted, and it was my job as a newly ordained deacon to find them in the prayer book as swiftly as possible.

He taught me to just come and sit and listen and sometimes hold his hand. It was not important that I say anything, and probably it was better if I didn't, just listen. As his illness progressed, I learned so much about him, especially from his family. He had very definite ideas about more than ecclesiastical matters and was vocal about them as well. He was constantly sending me emails and articles about issues, hoping to keep me well informed. Our politics were more than 180 degrees apart. A week before he died, he asked my views from a medical standpoint on the last article he gave me, the *National Review*'s "An End to Marijuana Prohibition."

We talked about writing our own book together about pastoral care, a kind of point, counterpoint. He had been on the giving and now the receiving end of pastoral visiting. He especially wanted to write a chapter on patients' rights and what they don't have to give up as they die. Patients can tell the lab not to come before six, tell the nurses to forget the late night vitals, tell the respiratory therapist who is impatient that he might send someone else in his place the next time.

Most of those who cared for him were beyond kindness and caring. Not just their words, but their body movements showed love, the way a nurse would gently reposition his pillow while he slept, or a doctor would put a hand on his shoulder while reading his chart. Their work was a ministry, not just a job. Staff would come in and tell him if they would be off the next day and that they would miss him. What a difference that kind of care can make.

The night he died we sat by his bed, held his hand with his family at his side, and watched a spectacular sunset. He mentioned, "You know I was supposed to die last night."

"Yes," I blurted out, "the reports of your demise have been greatly exaggerated!"

I quickly wondered if that was appropriate, but he laughed and so it seemed all right. I think that is the type of comment he would have made if he could have spoken such a long sentence.

His breathing was so labored. He had waited for his children to get there before he died. He wanted one last day with them. I watched him titrate his morphine so that he would be awake enough to be with his wife and children.

We all sat there for over an hour mostly in silence. We were alone for a few minutes while his family met visitors in the hall outside his room. He lifted our clasped hands and slowly spoke between deep breaths, "You have a healing touch." Just hours before he died, the one I came to minister to was instead ministering to me. I thanked him, and again he thanked me.

As I left, I whispered, "I will see you in the morning."

He slowly responded, "If I am still here."

I came back in the morning. His body was there at peace, no longer struggling with each breath. His beautiful spirit, however, is somewhere else, now empowered once again to speak out with the gift of clarity and conviction God gave to him. Most certainly he is now teaching and ministering to others as well as still to us.

He had planned his burial office to the last detail. He was to be cremated and his ashes placed in the columbarium, but he wanted his body at the service. A handmade, intricately-woven gold and white pall covered the coffin at the service. At the end of the burial office we followed the procession down a wooded path to the columbarium for the committal.

An unusual summer breeze rustled our white vestments as the crowd slowly and silently paced itself following the paschal candle and the cross. We reached the columbarium to find the elaborate pall had been removed. At this final resting place where we would say our last goodbyes and prayers was a simple pine box.

His presence was still there, teaching us one more lesson in truth and simplicity.

Prayer at the Committal While Earth is Cast Upon the Coffin:

In sure and certain hope of the resurrection to eternal life through our

Lord Jesus Christ, we commend to Almighty God our *brother*, and we commit *his* body to its resting place; earth to earth, ashes to ashes, dust to dust. The Lord bless *him* and keep *him*, the Lord make *his* face to shine upon *him* and be gracious unto *him*, the Lord lift up *his* countenance upon *him* and give *him* peace. Amen. —*BCP*, p. 485.

Progress not Perfection

"Two men went up into the temple to pray, one a Pharisee and the other a tax collector. The Pharisee stood and prayed thus with himself, 'God, I thank thee that I am not like other men'....But the tax collector standing far off, would not even lift up his eyes to heaven, but beat his breast, saying, 'God be merciful to me a sinner!'" Luke 18: 10-13.

They both died within twenty-four hours of each other. One died alone. There was rarely anyone else there the few times I visited. The other died surrounded by his family and many friends.

The death of the first was widely reported in the newspapers and on television. The other only had a very small obituary which appeared several days after he died.

The first man had spent a life of perfection, making certain that procedures were carried out precisely the right way. The second man had been an alcoholic for much of his life. He had an awakening in a recovery center seven years before he died. He spent the rest of his life helping others find and stay in recovery. His was a life of progress not perfection.

He died on his seventh AA birthday. That afternoon his AA friends brought a meeting to his house and gave him his seven-year AA coin. His daughter and his two grandchildren had made a birthday cake. The grandsons wanted to know why there was a number seven on Pops' birthday cake. "Isn't he 100 years old?" Pops laughed himself into a coughing fit when he heard that, as did all his other friends and family in his room.

After the meeting was over, he collapsed and died surrounded by those who loved him so dearly. His daughter writes: *Not a day goes by that we do not talk about him. The boys have asked if he will ever come back down from heaven.*

I learned so much from these two very great men. From the first, I had a secondhand experience of the price of being right, of the ending to a life lived demanding perfection in yourself and others. From all accounts, his life as well as his ending was in isolation and lonely. From the second man I learned what happens when we live a life of relationship, of progress, not perfection. There will always be community to support us if we are only open to that relationship and are aware and accepting of our own humanness as well as the imperfection in our neighbor who is just like us.

Daily we are given the choice of which life to try to live—progress or perfection.

A Prayer of St. Chrysostom

Almighty God, you have given us grace at this time with one accord to make our common supplication to you; and you have promised through your well-beloved Son that when two or three are gathered together in his Name you will be in the midst of them: Fulfill now, O Lord, our desires and petitions as may be best for us; granting us in this world knowledge of your truth, and in the age to come life everlasting. Amen. —*BCP*, p. 102.

IV.

JOURNEYS: WALKING THE ROAD TO EMMAUS

LUKE 24: 13-35

"As they came near the village to which they were going, he walked ahead as if he were going on. But they urged him strongly saying, 'Stay with us, because it is almost evening and the day is now nearly over.' So he went in to stay with them….Then their eyes were opened, and they recognized him."

"IN JERUSALEM DURING THE TIME OF KING SOLOMON, THERE WAS A SEPARATE PATH AROUND THE JEWISH TEMPLE FOR MOURNERS TO WALK. AS OTHERS IN THE COMMUNITY NOTICED THOSE IN GRIEF, THEY OFFERED SOLACE BY SAYING, 'MAY GOD COMFORT YOU AMONG THE MOURNERS OF ZION AND JERUSALEM.'"

—*Walking the Mourner's Path*, p. 2

Walking the Mourner's Path

"As they came near the village to which they were going, he walked ahead as if he were going on. But they urged him strongly saying, 'Stay with us, because it is almost evening and the day is now nearly over.' So he went in to stay with them… Then their eyes were opened, and they recognized him." Luke 24: 28-31.

My grandfather died almost thirty years ago. His was my most devastating loss. My career had moved me across the country, and I had not spent much time with him for the last ten years, but he was the one who loved me most unconditionally in my growing up years.

At his funeral, I cried uncontrollably. I walked by the rivers in my small hometown in Virginia after his service and prayed that I would stay connected to him and his love. I knew that I would not be able to survive unless I had hope that I would see my grandfather again. I wanted to believe desperately in the resurrection and life beyond our earthly death. My grandfather's love and death brought me back to the church and a longing for a relationship with God.

My father died five years later. I had promised my father that I would be with him when he died, but when the time came, I knew it was going to be too painful for me to be there. I had all kind of excuses for why I couldn't make it home as he came closer to dying. It took me months to work through the guilt of not being there.

My father left me a small inheritance. I had told him that I would use it for our children's college education. My father had always had a fantasy about becoming a beachcomber. I also love the beach. Shortly after his death we were led to look into purchasing some beach property.

We used our inheritance as a down payment. Over the last twenty years this place of solitude at the beach has strengthened our marriage and offered our family and friends a multitude of lifelong memories. As we walk on the beach and wait in anticipation for spectacular sunrises and sunsets over the ocean at this natural sanctuary, we continue to honor my father who continues to care for our family.

When my mother died I had an overwhelming feeling that suddenly I was free to become the person God had created me to be. Though my mother and I had a difficult relationship, I have no idea why I felt that way, for I never consciously felt that my mother had held me back from being or doing what I had wanted to be or do. Shortly after her death I was moved to seek ordination to the Diaconate. I think this would very much please my mother, but this was certainly not my motivation. Yet I realize now that she was instrumental in leading me to walk the path I was called to walk.

When my father-in-law died, we all experienced an extra dose of the Grace of God at his funeral. Our children on their own decided to bring pictures of their grandfather to his memorial service. Friends of his we had not seen for many years were there to honor him. The organist at his longtime Christian church played "For All the Saints" as the closing hymn. It was one of our favorite hymns, and certainly best described my father-in-law. We had not requested it, however, for we thought it was only an "Anglican" hymn. Grace is a gift given when you least expect it or have not asked for it. That day grace was photographs, old friends, and a favorite hymn reminding all of us of the life of a saint among us. A day does not go by that I do not think of the grace and faith that Bob taught me. Bob in his own illness taught me how to visit people who are sick. He helped me feel comfortable around the sick in nursing homes. I take his gentle spirit with me now each time I walk into a hospital visit.

The deaths of those I loved the deepest created life-changing revelations, midwifing me to go on new journeys to a new life and a new relationship to God, my family, and the world around me. I still feel their presence with me standing beside me and walking alongside me as I know they did in life. And as they are beside and alongside me, so is the presence of God.

Morning Service for the New Year

The soul which Thou, O God, hast given unto me came pure from Thee. Thou hast created it, Thou hast formed it, Thou hast breathed it into me; Thou has preserved it in this body and, at the appointed time, Thou wilt take it from this earth that it may enter upon life everlasting. While the breath of life is within me, I will worship Thee, Sovereign of the world and Lord of all souls. Praised be Thou, O God, in whose hands are the souls of all the living and the spirits of all flesh. —*Union Prayerbook for Jewish Worship*, p. 40.

For All the Saints

"Let us now sing the praises of famous men,
Our ancestors in their generations.
The Lord apportioned to them great glory,
His majesty from the beginning...
All these were honored in their generations,
And were the pride of their times.
Some of them have left behind a name,
So that others declare their praise,
But of others there is no memory." Ecclesiasticus 44: 1-9.

Jennifer calls to say her mother, Maud, has died. She has never been to a funeral before, much less planned one. We meet in her living room to say prayers for her mother and to go over the service in the prayer book.

As I prepare, I give thanks for those before us who have planned prayers and scriptures in our prayer book. This is early in my pastoral care experience, and I have only planned two other funerals: my own mother's service, and the funeral of a friend. I give thanks for priests who led me through both of these preparations. I give thanks for their concern and tenderness. I have had two wonderful role models. I pray that God will allow me to remember their sensitivity and not be hardened by the ordinariness of death.

Jennifer is still grieving her father's death several years earlier. Even after two years I still grieve my own mother's death. Can I keep this sensitivity in front of me and be present in the pain of planning this funeral today? It is for someone I do not know, but her daughter is one of the original members of our church.

I feel the presence of so many who have done this before us. I feel the presence of saints who are standing or sitting on the couch beside the two of us. Their presence is in the words of the prayers and in the scripture and in the form of the service. I am more aware that we only know the names of a few who have formed the service in the *Book of Common Prayer.* "Of others there is no memory." But their presence is still here. I feel it.

I feel the presence of friends who have died. They are here giving us the words to say and comforting Jennifer. In brief moments, I can even see the bright eyes and smiles of Nyna and Dodie, other dear friends who have died, who tell us to have no fear.

The peace of God that Maud now knows is indescribable. They have all come to be with us to share that peace and give us a little glimpse of what it is like so that we will be comforted.

As we sit close by each other on the couch, we review once again each detail of the service. Just before leaving I look up at the calendar to record the day and time of Maud's funeral. I suddenly stop as I look at the date and chills run down my spine as I see God's grace working one more detail.

I look to Jennifer and her eyes are filled with the same joy. Her mother's memorial service will be on November first, All Saint's Day.

Prayer at Burial

Almighty God, with whom still live the spirits of those who die in the

Lord, and with whom the souls of the faithful are in joy and felicity: We give you heartfelt thanks for the good examples of all your servants, who having finished their course in faith, now find rest and refreshment. May we, with all who have died in the true faith of your holy Name, have perfect fulfillment and bliss in your eternal and everlasting glory; through Jesus Christ our Lord. Amen. —*BCP*, p. 503.

Carrying on Her Spirit

"When they had crossed, Elijah said to Elisha, 'Tell me what I may do for you, before I am taken from you.' Elisha said, 'Please let me inherit a double share of you spirit.'" 2 Kings 2: 9.

Virginia died today in her ninety-first year. She had been a founding member of our church. She was seventy-six when she came as a missionary member to help start St. Margaret's.

We came to know her the best in her eighty-seventh year when she decided to join our Education for Ministry (EFM) class. What a treasure to have in the group someone with this sense of history and walk with God for almost a century. When each of us in our class did our timeline spiritual autobiography, she gave us a depth and width that none of us had experienced. She continually encouraged us to see how God was working in our lives. It was a privilege just to sit beside her.

Her Christmas present from one of her daughters was to have a tea at her home for our class as her daughter and her husband and a friend played traditional and Celtic Christmas music in her living room. I cannot think of a soul who did not love her.

And of course there were her grandchildren who especially had a sense of how special they were to have this gracious and grateful lady as their "Din." They sobbed like none other at her death.

The night of her death one granddaughter recited to her the prayer Virginia always read to them when they spent the night with her. The granddaughter could not remember the last lines. Virginia, just a few hours before dying, recited the conclusion of the poem when Mary Starr hesitated: "The stars are watching overhead./Sleep sweetly then, goodnight."

I constantly realize that as people die, those who hear the news often say, "Oh, I was just going over to see or call today." There are always regrets about not being there or what we did not do. This is universal. We keep remembering what we did not do. That was my case as well. I had heard that Virginia was not well last night, but when we took food by her house that night we heard that she had rallied at the hospital. I woke early this morning and planned to go to visit at daybreak. Then the call came that she had died later in the night.

I so wanted to be with Virginia at her death, for the presence of God seemed to surround her. I wanted to say prayers for preparation for death with her, for I knew they would be meaningful to her. I also realized that my being with her was more for me than for her. I knew she would be surrounded by a huge, loving family. She would not be alone. I was longing personally to have one more time to say goodbye, one more chance just to be in her presence.

I kept thinking back to last night. What was keeping me from going? I had planned an evening with our granddaughter, Langley. We went by Virginia's house to take food to her family on our way out to eat, then to a play and finally arrived home late. Suddenly it came to me. I think this is what Virginia would have wanted me to do. She so valued her grandchildren, and they so loved her. What better way to honor her than to be with one of my precious grandchildren as Virginia died.

I hope I can remember this beautiful role model I have had the privilege of being with, a role model of what is important in life, of how to give and receive God's love. I am learning this is how to honor those who have died, to carry on the love and ministry we have learned from them that they now transfer to us.

Two days later our almost five-year-old granddaughter goes to visit her other grandparents. She tells her other grandmother that her grandparents in Little Rock have a friend named Virginia who is very old and very sick and she would like to write her a note. Langley's mother then tells her that actually Virginia has died, but what she could do is write a note to Virginia's daughter, Starr, who played music at her mother and daddy's wedding.

How connected we all are, and how often it takes a child to show us.

Sleep sweetly in this quiet room
Oh thou, whoe'er thou art,
And let no mournful yesterdays
Disturb thy peaceful heart.
Nor let tomorrow scare thy rest
With thoughts of coming ill.
Thy maker is thy changeless friend.
His love surrounds thee still.
Forget thyself and all the world.
Put out each feverish light.
The stars are watching overhead.
Sleep sweetly then, goodnight.

—Victor Hugo

Virginia

Four Marys

"Meanwhile, standing near the cross of Jesus were his mother, and his mother's sister, Mary the wife of Clopas, and Mary Magdalene. When Jesus saw his mother and the disciple whom he loved standing beside her, he said to his mother, 'Woman, here is your son.' Then he said to the disciple, 'Here is your Mother.' And from that hour the disciple took her into his own home." John 19: 26-27.

Two weeks after her daughter's funeral, I met Mary for coffee. Anne had been killed in a tragic train accident in another country the summer before she was to enter college.

It was an unusually cool summer morning. I felt Mary in the room before I even saw her. After a tearful hug we began talking about Anne's funeral. We marveled at the number of friends Anne had and the people she had touched in her young life. We went over all the details of the glorious celebration of Anne's life: the music, the choir, the liturgy, the reception and how no one wanted to leave.

Mary then began slowly to talk about the new directions she already felt in her life. She told me how she had spent much time trying not to wear masks in her life, but that this great loss had made her even more desiring of not being anything that was false to her. She was living her life one day at a time. She was not making a lot of plans and was trying to be open to what God had in store for her that day.

She also had a vision of what her life's mission should be: to become the person God had intended her to be with all her heart. Mary was not certain what that was, but she was more open than she ever had known. She spoke of feeling God's presence and support throughout this entire tragedy. She wondered how anyone could survive such a loss without the love and faith in God.

Then she could barely speak as she softly whispered that she had some insight into the thoughts of our Lord's mother, another Mary, at the cross.

Mary then looked away from me and at the cars passing by in the busy street close to our table. As we sat in silence, I could not help being overwhelmed with thoughts of how awful the loss of a child must be. It is unimaginable. Parents should not have to bury their children. My mind filled with images of parents of children I have known in my work at Children's Hospital who have sat by bedsides as their children have suffered and died. There was love, protection, caring, sorrow, anger, comfort, helplessness, and surrender, as I have never seen in any other situations.

Mary's eyes once again met mine, and I was overwhelmed with the love and faith that shone back from within. She held out her hand and took mine in hers, enveloping mine with her warmth.

Prayer for Those Who Mourn at Time of Death

Almighty God, look with pity upon the sorrows of your servants for whom we pray. Remember them, Lord, in mercy; nourish them with patience; comfort them with a sense of your goodness; lift up your countenance upon them; and give them peace; through Jesus Christ our Lord. Amen. —BCP, p. 467.

Anne Receiving Award in Religion at Her School

Breakfast with Gay

"Just after daybreak, Jesus stood on the beach; but the disciples did not know that it was Jesus. Jesus said to them, 'Children, you have no fish, have you?' … When they had gone ashore, they saw a charcoal fire there, with fish on it and bread. Jesus said to them, '…. Come and have breakfast.' Now none of the disciples dared to ask him, 'Who are you?' because they knew it was the Lord. This was the third time that Jesus appeared to the disciples after he was raised from the dead." John 21: 4-14.

We meet for coffee two weeks after her husband died. He was to retire that month. She had spent the last year wondering how they would adjust to his retirement. Now Gay has to adjust to his physical absence from her life. Her own mother had suffered with dementia for four years. During this time, Gay had become mother to her own mother. But just for a brief moment, when her mother heard of Frank's death, she became Gay's mother again. "Gay, I know you will really miss, Frank," she said as only a mother could say to her daughter.

We meet again a month later. Gay has just returned from a hiking trip out west. She had planned the trip for some time with her niece and decided to go ahead and go. It was met with many challenges. Forest fires kept them from most of the hiking trails. They decided to go shopping. Gay is not a big shopper. She saw an outfit that was perfect for her, but more expensive than what she usually buys. She gets it but keeps wondering, "Can I afford it now that I have a single income? What would Frank think?" As they leave the shop, Gay's niece points to a sign in the window: *Your husband has called and said you could buy anything you wanted.*

We meet again two months later for breakfast. We can begin to laugh about all this, but I know it is still very difficult. As we are ready to leave, our waitress tells us someone has paid for our breakfast. A gentleman comes over and tells Gay, "I so admired your husband and wanted to do something to honor him for his wonderful life. When I saw you this morning, I knew I could start by paying for your breakfast."

We look at each other and smile, knowing that instead of absent, Frank is very much present.

Collect After the Laying on of Hands

May the God who goes before you through desert places by night and by day be your companion and guide; may your journey be with the saints; may the Holy Spirit be your strength, and Christ your clothing of light, in whose name we pray. Amen. —*Enriching Your Worship 2*, p. 53.

Frank

Easter on Ash Wednesday

"When you give a luncheon or a dinner, do not invite your friends or your brothers or your relatives or rich neighbors, in case they may invite you in return, and you would be repaid. But when you give a banquet, invite the poor, the crippled, the lame, and the blind. And you will be blessed, because they cannot repay you, for you will be repaid at the resurrection of the righteous." Luke 14: 12-14.

Six weeks ago on Ash Wednesday we attended the funeral of the father of one of my dearest friends. Barbara's Dad had died in his ninety-ninth year. I was moved during the funeral service at the Methodist church that Doc had attended as each member of Barbara's family participated in the celebration of his life. I was most affected as our families walked together in the misty rain to the burial place of his ashes in the wooded grounds that would be the future home of St. Margaret's Episcopal Church. I had never before been to a burial in the woods. "Dust to Dust" had new meaning in those natural surroundings on that cool Ash Wednesday that we all silently knew we would always remember.

When we returned to Hap and Barbara's home, we were greeted by members of St. Paul's Methodist Church who brought dinner. None of us knew these people from St. Paul's Care Team. Neither did any of them know Doc, for he had not been able to attend his church for several years. They were older men and women, and we later learned all had lost a significant loved one. We were strangers who could never directly repay their kindness. They were so gentle and knew exactly what to say, how to console, how long to stay. They had a glow I cannot describe. Here were a group of people who had suffered through great pain and death. I wondered how long each gentle face I could remember had been separated from his or her loved one. How long did their pain last? Were some still hurting and lonely? But in their pain they had found a new life and were now reaching out to strangers with some of the same hurting.

It is now Easter morning, and I sit in the Columbarium at St. Marks and pray, just as I have for the past several years, that I will know the Risen Lord. I walk into the sanctuary. It is quiet in the church now, but soon it will be filled with triumphant music and singing and children and families. As I stare at the white lilies on the altar, my thoughts go to that Wednesday at Hap and Barbara's home. As I think back on that day, I suddenly realize the glow coming from within the members of St. Paul's Care Team was a tiny glimpse of the resurrection. That is resurrection—a new life born out of great pain and death. I saw it demonstrated in lives of the living.

For me this year God has not followed the liturgical calendar. This year I experienced Easter on Ash Wednesday.

Prayer for the Absent

O God, whose fatherly care reaches to the uttermost parts of the earth: We humbly beseech thee graciously to behold and bless those whom we love, now absent from us. Defend them from all dangers of soul and body; and grant that both they and we, drawing nearer to thee, may be bound together by thy love in the communion of thy Holy Spirit, and in the fellowship of thy saints; through Jesus Christ our Lord. Amen. —*BCP*, p. 830.

Doc

Until Death Us Do Part

"Arise, my love, my fair one, and come away. Set me as a seal upon your heart, as a seal upon your arm; for love is strong as death, passion fierce as the grave. Its flashes are flashes of fire, a raging flame. Many waters cannot quench love, neither can floods drown it." Song of Solomon 2: 10; 8: 6-7.

It was to be their eleventh wedding anniversary. She had died ten months ago, but the deep pain was still raw. We met in the Cathedral where they had been married.

It was a bright Saturday morning, just like their wedding day. His children had sent flowers to be placed in front of the altar. Behind the altar were even more flowers for the wedding of another friend's son that evening. We sat in the choir stalls. We then gathered around the high altar at the church triumphant and said prayers. We all spoke about the loss we still felt and the memories that were still so real.

He had brought a box with her wedding ring in it. He said a prayer and then took off his wedding band and placed it beside hers. Until death us do part.

We stayed a while longer, and then stepped out of the Cathedral and into the bright sunlight. We got into our separate cars and then drove to lunch at a place he had never eaten before. And as we ate, we told more stories.

Blessing at a Marriage

God the Father, God the Son, God the Holy Spirit, bless, preserve, and keep you; the Lord mercifully with his favor look upon you, and fill you with all spiritual benediction and grace; that you may faithfully live together in this life, and in the age to come have life everlasting. Amen.
—*BCP*, p. 431.

St. Lucy's Day

"In the beginning was the Word, and the Word was with God, and the Word was God. He was in the beginning with God. All things came into being through him, and without him not one thing came into being. What has come into being in him was life, and the life was the light of all people. The light shines in the darkness, and the darkness did not overcome it." John 1: 1-5.

We gathered at the exact time Jane died a year ago. Her husband Pat, her best friend Carol, my husband, and another priest stood in the snow in the columbarium by her ashes on this St. Lucy's day.

Like Jane, Lucy was a brave spiritual woman who had had a premature death. I kept thinking back to this day a year ago. I was not able to be with Jane when she died. I remember how I had wanted to help prepare her body and do all the loving things that should be done by people who love you so much. I knew there were family members and friends there who did do that, but I longed to be that part of goodbyes to her.

Through the months that followed, I realized helping with this service at the columbarium on the anniversary of her death would allow us all to say some of these goodbyes we still carried.

Carol brought pink roses. We said Psalms, read from John, Romans, and Revelation. Pat read a letter to Jane. He talked about how the physician who pronounced her death put it at 8:37am, but she really had died at 8:27am. Carol told how she had tried to correct the doctor, but the physician had told her, "She isn't dead until I say so." Pat reminded us that the world had given her ten more minutes than she really had to live, and how he wished medical science could have given her ten more years.

We cried, laughed, and hugged and then went to breakfast.

Pat and Carol talked about what the first year after losing a spouse was like. They shared how the greatest grief was in the little things. Pat still was moved when he saw Jane's handwriting. Carol remembered having to change a light bulb in the ceiling she had never done before her first husband, Lynn, died. Pat talked about using every day a special eyeglass cleaner that Jane had prepared especially for him.

Suddenly as they talked I remembered that St. Lucy's name in Latin means "light" and that she is the patron saint of those who are blind or have poor eyesight.

Pat and Carol further shared what great comfort others who have also been through the grief process were to them. It was not the books that so many people had given them to read that had helped, but the people themselves who shared their light and their darkness, their presence and their stories. They both reaffirmed their faith and wondered how people without a spiritual family survive.

It was almost noon when we said our goodbyes and left the restaurant to go home that unusually cold winter morning. We all rode away knowing that we had been on the receiving end of grace. We had heard and experienced the light, love and wisdom that are born from wounded-ness and loss.

Collect After Laying on of Hands

God of all mercy: help us who minister with the sick and dying to remember that though we may appear healthy, we, too, suffer from the universal human condition in a fallen world, and we must all die to the life we know. Therefore, O God our help, teach us to be aware of our own infirmities, the better to make others understand they are not alone in their illness. Restore us all in the love of the holy and undivided Trinity which is our true health and salvation. Amen.

—*Enriching Our Worship 2*, p. 40.

Dream House

"Everyone then who hears these words of mine and acts on them will be like a wise man who built his house on rock. The rain fell, the floods came, and the winds blew and beat on that house, but it did not fall, because it had been founded on rock." Matthew 7: 24-25.

It has been almost two years now since Jane has died. The house is too big for just one person. It was their dream house they had spent years planning. She was only able to live in it for one and a half years, and for the last six months she had been ill. Pat found a smaller house nearby just right for one person.

A beautiful family with two small children fell in love with Jane's house. The father is a philosophy professor and is immediately drawn to the huge library and study that Jane had planned and designed for Pat. His wife loves to cook and sees all the love in Jane's kitchen and sitting area adjacent to it. The children immediately find Jane's secret loft playroom she had designed for her grandchildren.

We come to the house for the last time and say prayers of thanksgiving for the beautiful life and memories of the house and say prayers for the new family who will soon be living there. We end our ritual outside in the side yard of their house. Pat has brought a rock with Jane's name on it that has been the symbol of his marriage during his grief recovery group called the Mourner's Path. He buries the rock by a tree that came from Jane's childhood home.

We then get into our cars and follow Pat the short distance to his new home. We go from room to room and participate in the blessing of a new house. We then sit down in the new dining room and share the first supper in this new house. It is a holy evening full of tears and laughter and old and new life.

Prayer for Those Who Live Alone

Almighty God, whose Son had nowhere to lay his head: Grant that those who live alone may not be lonely in their solitude, but that, following in his steps, they may find fulfillment in loving you and their neighbors; through Jesus Christ our Lord. Amen. —*BCP*, p. 829.

V.

MEETING ANGELS UNAWARE

HEBREWS 13: 1-2

"Let mutual love continue. Do not neglect to show hospitality to strangers, for by doing that some have entertained angels without knowing it."

"MEDICINE GAINED ME ENTRANCE TO THE SECRET GARDENS OF THE SELF. I WAS PERMITTED BY MY MEDICAL BADGE TO FOLLOW THE POOR, DEFEATED BODY INTO THOSE GULFS AND GROTTOS."

—William Carlos Williams

Reunions

"Let mutual love continue. Do not neglect to show hospitality to strangers, for by doing that some have entertained angels without knowing it." Hebrews: 13: 1-2.

I so well remember the day my husband Robert retired from his medical practice and his patients returned to say thank you and good-bye. His primary work had been operating on children with cleft palates and lips, restoring these children to a life of beauty and hope. It was so moving to see the gratitude of these children and their parents for his work.

I knew this was an experience that I would only know secondhand, through him, for my medical specialty is pediatric radiology. Most of the patients I help never know or see me or the work I have done to help restore them to health. It is the downside of being in a medical specialty where you deal more with other physicians than with patients.

However, I had a monumental experience recently when I attended the twenty-fifth birthday of the neonatal unit at Children's Hospital. I had been at Children's when the neonatal intensive care unit had been born. Patients and their parents who had been cared for in this intensive care unit returned to celebrate this great anniversary. I was in a room filled with children most of whose X-rays I had read, on whom I had performed many procedures. Some I knew I had helped care for and diagnose their condition. The children and their parents would not know me, and I would never know them. Most of my prayers for them had been in secret, as I learned to know their inner being only in the black and white of their X-rays.

But there was an overwhelming feeling of being in a room full of people whom I had known intimately and had in some small way walked beside them on a journey in the first days of their lives. Perhaps sometimes I helped them, restored them to life, or had given them a new life. We would never know each other.

I cried with joy. I knew life had some meaning as I saw these children, many now adults. I knew God had used me for a purpose, often when I had forgotten about it or was unaware. It did not matter that we did not recognize each other. We had a beautiful secret bond of helping each other on this journey.

I saw angels unaware. I had the rare opportunity of seeing seeds that I had sown and now witnessed these beautiful fruits of the spirit.

Bless, O Lord, your gifts to our use and us to your service; for Christ's sake. Amen. —BCP, p. 835.

Robert and His Patients at His Retirement

Teachers

"People were bringing little children to him in order that he might touch them; and the disciples spoke sternly to them. But when Jesus saw this, he was indignant and said to them, 'Let the little children come to me; do not stop them; for it is to such as these that the kingdom of God belongs. Truly I tell you, whoever does not receive the kingdom of God as a little child will never enter it.' And he took them up in his arms, laid his hands on them, and blessed them." Mark 10: 13-16.

He lay there on the X-ray table waiting for his procedure to begin. He was silent, but elephant tears were welling up in his eyes. He was fourteen, but the size of a nine-year-old. Less subtle scars ran across his tummy. He had struggled with cancer and its complications for most of his life.

Today we would be investigating another possible complication of his disease. I saw in his face an awareness of life far beyond his age. His mother sat by him. She rarely spoke. Had she been numbed by his years of struggle, or had she struggled so long that she now was at a place of acceptance of whatever might come?

I was in a hurry. I had an important luncheon to make. This was not an easy case, not the sort of problem to work out on the run.

A moment of grace allowed this haunting face to speak to me. That grace told me to stop, take off my shoes, and glimpse the holy that was at an altar before me. This young African American boy, wise beyond his years, had known life at a magnitude beyond any of my awareness. I had been called to serve, to help in any way possible to relieve even a little of his suffering. I touched the hand of this young boy. He now had become my teacher, silently whispering to me what life, work, relationships were all about. Luncheons, meetings were no longer on the agenda.

A few weeks later, my medical partners and I learn from another teacher what our profession and work is all about. The child of one of my partners develops cancer. We see her daily struggle with her son for survival. We see the constant visits back to the hospital, the year her son is out of school, the weeks of chemotherapy, the surgery, the wound that will not heal for months, the constant tests, the bad reports, the good reports. We see this daily from one single person rather than in little bits and pieces from many patients.

I begin to be more aware of members of our department who constantly emulate the caring concern that is so easy for me to lose in the daily grind of getting the work done. Our pediatric radiology nurse Dorcas tenderly treats each child like her own. The nuclear medicine and ultrasound technologists seem never to lose their sense of their true ministry. They carefully talk with each patient and their parents to make sure they know what is going on each moment during their tests. They use all their knowledge available to find answers to what is going on with each patient presented to them. They concentrate on each child and give them the care they would want their own to have. They grieve when their patients do not get well and rejoice when they return to health. Like an alarm clock, they daily shock me back to the reality that this is the way I should be acting as well.

I need to spend more time with them and hear their secrets. Maybe when I am not so busy and have a little more time.

For today I will just watch how they act and hope our patients and those I work with won't give up teaching me what our ministry at this children's hospital is all about.

Prayer for Doctors and Nurses

Sanctify, O Lord, those whom you have called to the study and practice of the arts of healing, and to the prevention of disease and pain. Strengthen them by your life-giving Spirit, that their ministries may promote the health of the community and your creation glorified; through Jesus Christ our Lord. Amen. —BCP, p. 460.

Friday Afternoon

"We also boast in our suffering, knowing that suffering produces endurance, and endurance produces character, and character produces hope, and hope does not disappoint us, because God's love has been poured into our hearts through the Holy Spirit that has been given to us." Romans 5: 3-5.

It is 4:45pm on Friday. I have fifteen minutes left before I go home from a long day at work. I am ready to leave and have a big evening planned. The day has been rewarding. I spent time teaching, taking care of patients, and may have even helped someone.

The ultrasound tech comes in with a difficult scan she has just performed. She shows the case to one of my partners, who then asks if someone else can do it, for he is tied up. I look at it. It doesn't look good. The patient is a two-year-old little boy. His mother is concerned that her son's tummy looks too big and hard. She has an appointment to see us on Monday, but almost hysterically called to see if she could come in this afternoon. She is very concerned.

I go back to look again with our ultrasound tech. The mother is crying. She has a friend with her. As we look, all I can see is what looks like tumor filling his tummy.

I tell the mother, "I am seeing these masses. We need to do more tests to see what they are."

His mother's friend asks, "What do you mean by masses?"

I say, "I am worried about a tumor. We must do more tests."

Jason's mother becomes hysterical. "My husband died a year ago from cancer. I can't lose my little boy."

I try to comfort her, but there are not words. "I am sorry. We just need more tests."

I call her pediatrician's office and am on hold for almost ten minutes before I get to her. We get some more X-rays, and then I walk them over to the Emergency Department for admission. The Emergency Room is full; there are no beds in the hospital, for this is RSV season. A major trauma has just rolled in the door. I find the admitting physician. She finds a little space for them.

As I leave the mother's friend whispers in my ear, "Her husband recently died. Every time you say you are sorry, you make her feel worse."

As I leave, I tell the admitting physician the situation and how little I have been able to help them. I am now late for dinner with my family and a meeting at church.

I offer prayers for this family and think about them all weekend. I am depressed how little I had to offer and the negative feedback. My medical experience tells me that the road ahead is very bleak for this mother and her child. There will be much more suffering and an overwhelming chance of a painful death for her beloved son. I see nothing but sadness and death ahead. Where is the endurance, character, hope, and love that comes with suffering?

I visit them on Monday morning. It is a new day. The mother hugs me and thanks me for helping her child. She knows that the road ahead will be difficult. Her own mother and her friend are at her side, holding her hand and Jason's. My experience now reminds me that hope rises strongest in those who do not suffer in isolation. When we lose all hope, God sends it to us in our friends. When we suffer together, God becomes present in the arms of those who let us rest in them.

What also comes back in my prayers for this family is, "It's not all about you." I begin to have some sense of offering the best skills I have, knowing that sometimes I will get positive feedback and sometimes negative. My job is to stay as alert as possible to do this and realize that I am only one of many of God's instruments.

Will I ever learn how to stand in the face of others without having to take up all the space?

Holy Spirit, free us from our idealized image of ourselves which over-reacts to daily life with feelings of self-exaltation or self-depreciation. Guide us to a true and humble knowledge and acceptance of who we really are and how to do your will always. Amen.

The Orderly

"Jesus was praying in a certain place, and after he had finished, one of his disciples said to him, 'Lord, teach us to pray, as John taught his disciples.' He said to them, 'When you pray, say 'Father, hallowed be your name. Your kingdom come. Give us each day our daily bread. And forgive us our sins, for we ourselves forgive everyone indebted to us. And do not bring us to the time of trial.'" Luke 11: 1-4.

I had promised I would come and say prayers before his surgery. I was running late. William's surgery was at one o'clock.

I arrived at twelve thirty just behind the African American orderly who was to take him to surgery. They may be called something differently today, transport team or stat team, but I knew him as an orderly. William looked so glad to see me. Internally I said a thank you prayer for just getting me there.

I asked the orderly if we had time for prayers. He said, "Of course." I asked him if he would like to pray with us. I anointed William with oil and then we prayed.

The power of prayer coming from the orderly now leaning over Williams's bed was beyond belief. I have never seen anything quite like it. He was earnestly praying for someone he had just met for the first time. His whole body and soul were in the prayers we said together.

Then the orderly led us to the operating suite, and I stayed with William until he went into surgery. The orderly then not only showed me where to wait but walked with me to the waiting room.

I learned so much this day, how to pray, how to live your life as a ministry.

Of course, I did not learn the orderly's name. How I wish I had done so that I could let his supervisors know what a gift they had.

Prayer for the Answering of Prayer

Almighty God, who hast promised to hear the petitions of those who ask in thy Son's Name: We beseech thee mercifully to incline thine ear to us who have now made our prayers and supplications unto thee; and grant that those things which we have faithfully asked according to thy will, may effectually be obtained, to the relief of our necessity, and to the setting forth of thy glory; through Jesus Christ our Lord. Amen. — BCP, p. 834.

First Day Back

"Those who eat my flesh and drink my blood have eternal life, and I will raise them up on the last day..." John 6: 53-59.

Sadness spills out of every pore of her body. It is our resident's first day back at work after her father's death. Yvonne has just returned from her parents' home in Texas late the night before. She and her father were very close. He also was a radiologist and her lifelong role model.

She can barely speak she is so fragile. Almost inaudibly she says, "I thought I could do this, but I don't see how I can make it through this day."

We sit down in front of viewing boxes of X-rays. But instead of reading the films in front of us, we talk about her father, she cries, and then we seek distraction in our work. We talk again, she cries, and then we read more X-rays together.

Memories flood through my own mind of the first days after my father died over fifteen years earlier. I remember how I wanted to say to each person I met, "Did you know that my father has died?" It was too hard to comprehend that the world could keep going on business as usual when I had just lost my father.

The most significant person in my growing up years was my Baptist grandfather. When he died over twenty years ago, I was devastated almost as much as Yvonne is now. I think back and try to recall what helped me the most get through that sadness and loss.

I remember that I was moved to do something to honor my grandfather and his life. I was a long time heavy smoker, the equivalent of a pack a day for twenty years. I can still see my grandfather's loving eyes and hear his deep voice, "I wish so much that you did not smoke. I saw my own mother, your great grandmother, die of tuberculosis. I don't want to see someone else so dear to me die from lung disease." I tried to stop many times but never was able to do so. I knew my quitting smoking would please my grandfather.

By some miracle, I was given that grace and have not smoked a cigarette since December 7, 1979, the day of his funeral. It was a miracle, a real spiritual healing. My grandfather not only showed me unconditional love in its truest form while he lived, but now even in death is still caring for me by literally saving my life.

The spirit of my grandfather gave me the strength to do something I had never been able to do before. Those who have died, those in eternal life, are constantly with us in spirit to comfort and guide and love us as much and maybe sometimes even more than when they were living.

I think of Leigh Ann Bennett, a member of our congregation who is presently a fourth year psychiatry resident. Two and half years ago her father, also a radiologist, tragically committed suicide. Leigh Ann worked through her own grief by helping to spearhead a foundation to educate people, especially in White County, about depression and its signs and symptoms. Our medical school recently honored her for that work with the Joycelyn Elders award for community service. After her first child is born, Leigh Ann plans to speak at our church, St. Margaret's, educating us as well about suicide and depression.

I shared some of these stories with Yvonne. She, too, has already thought of honoring her father. Her eyes brighten and color returns to her face as she tells me, "My father took the Eucharist to patients in a nursing home in my hometown in Texas every Saturday on his day off. He took out the sacraments the day before he died. I have this strong desire to continue his Eucharistic ministry either there or here in Little Rock."

Suddenly memories of my mother's death just one year earlier flood through my consciousness. I wanted to take Eucharist to my mother in the hospital but did not make it home in time. I then remember the day I returned to Little Rock after my mother's funeral. A friend calls, "Can you bring Eucharist to the hospital to my mother? By some miracle she is beginning to recover from a near death illness." Later at the bedside I am strangely warmed as I observe a physical resemblance between my friend's mother and my own mother. I am reminded of how God often comforts us by allowing us to serve other loved ones when we can not, for unknown reasons, be with our most immediate loved ones.

Later in the afternoon that day at Children's Hospital, Yvonne and I go to the neonatal intensive care nursery to evaluate a very sick newborn. As we start to perform our examination we realize that the mother who is at the bedside is Mexican and cannot speak or understand English. She has been at her baby's side all day long not knowing what is going on with her very ill one-day-old son.

Yvonne looks into the frightened and confused eyes of this mother and whispers, "*Yo hablo Espanol.*" Our resident speaks fluent Spanish because she is from south Texas and because her father was an immigrant from Spain. "*Su hijo esta' muy enfermo.*" She then tenderly begins to interpret our findings, explaining exactly what we are doing and describing to that young mother the serious condition of her beloved infant.

As I watch Yvonne stand beside the new mother and reach out and take her hand, I realize that Christ is reaching out to heal us from our losses, recent and past. God uses a young physician in great emotional pain who still is able to reach out to a young mother also in great distress. They will probably never meet again, but they have a glimpse of the Christ, *el Christo*, abiding in each other. They have a glimpse of the shape of each other's heart.

As our day together ends we both reflect through red eyes and cracking voices what a difficult day this has been, but how amazing it is how God reaches out to comfort our pain in places and through people we least expect.

This is the wisdom we are taught in the "synagogue" of Children's Hospital. The death of someone we love is not a period at the end of a sentence, but more like a comma, where the one we love is not only in a new relationship with God, but also in a new love relationship with us as well.

* * *

It has been two years since that day with Yvonne. Yesterday I sent her an email asking permission to tell her story. This is her reply:

I remember this day as if it were yesterday, though two and a half years have passed, and with time and prayer, healing.

One of the things you told me that day was that I would think of and feel the presence my dad more now that he is gone, than had he been physically present. How true that is! No emotion is spared thoughts of him—happy, sad, anxious. One occasion in particular I wanted to share with you the day it happened, but, despite good intentions, offered up a prayer rather than a phone call. Now you have given me the opportunity to share it.

On my birthday this past year, I woke up, of course, with thoughts of my dad. I went to church and on my way out heard the hurried footsteps of Sr. Dorothy, a nun/nurse with whom I had become friends through my persistence in trying to get involved with this local church. Would you believe, she asked me if I would be interested in becoming a Eucharistic minister! On my birthday! What a gift! I walked home with my emotions 180 degrees turned from what they had been, filled with peace and joy and undeniably feeling the presence of God right in step with me. Never abandoned!! Thanks for my Dad! Thanks be to God!

Prayer for the Bereaved

Grant, O Lord, to all who are bereaved the spirit of faith and courage, that they may have strength to meet the days to come with steadfastness and patience; not sorrowing as those without hope, but in thankful remembrance of your great goodness, and in the joyful expectation of eternal life with those they love. And this we ask in the Name of Jesus Christ our Savior. Amen. —*BCP*, p. 505.

Death of a Son

"See what love the Father has given us, that we should be called children of God; and that is what we are. The reason the world does not know us is that it did not know him. Beloved, we are God's children now; what we will be has not yet been revealed. What we do know is this: when he is revealed, we will be like him, for we will see him as he is." 1 John 3: 1-2.

We are saddened to hear of the death of a patient my husband and I both cared for. We knew a little of his suffering and his love of life and his courage. He was close to our sons' ages. In fact he knew one of our sons. We in some small way identify with the pain his parents must feel. We cannot imagine the grief one bears in losing a child. I am reminded of other women who have lost sons as we attend a performance of Euripides' Suppliant Women. There must be no description for their pain. It seems it was no less senseless or less intense more than 2000 years ago as our civilization began. I feel Good Friday pain.

We are out of town for the funeral. I go to a quiet chapel on a college campus during the time of the service looking for connection. I see the flowers at the altar from the previous Easter Sunday. I feel a little glimmer of hope. Suddenly the chapel becomes even brighter and less quiet as large bouquets of flowers are brought in by a group of very busy women. They are preparing the church for a wedding that afternoon.

Their preparation is moving, sacred. I feel almost simultaneously the sorrow of death and the excitement of new life—the continual paradox of this life.

I have a choice. I can isolate myself and retreat from pain by refusing to stay in relationship with patients, family or friends, or by numbing my mind and body with the multitude of life's possibilities that can keep me from feeling when the feelings are so intense.

Today in this chapel I once again choose the paradox. I pray for those bearing more pain than I, that they be allowed to feel and express their pain, but that they too will be lifted up by signs of a new life or the preparations for it.

Prayer at Burial

Father of all, we pray to you for those we love, but see no longer: Grant them your peace; let light perpetual shine upon them; and, in your loving wisdom and almighty power, work in them the good purpose of your perfect will; through Jesus Christ our Lord. Amen.
—*BCP*, p. 504.

Miracles on Marshall Street

"Now there was a woman who had been suffering from hemorrhages for twelve years. She had endured much under many physicians, and had spent all that she had; and she was no better, but rather grew worse. She heard about Jesus, and came up behind him in the crowd and touched his cloak. For she said, 'If I but touch his clothes, I will be made well.' Immediately her hemorrhage stopped; and she felt in her body that she was healed of her disease. Immediately aware that power had gone forth from him, Jesus turned about in the crowd and said, 'Who touched my clothes?'" Mark 5: 25-30.

It is Wednesday evening, and I am sitting in our X-ray reading room looking on the hospital computer for laboratory results on a young girl who just had a kidney transplant that we examined earlier in the day.

It has been a hectic week. On Monday I had been consulted about a child with a possible fracture about the face from a significant fall. I thought he might have a fracture around the eye and recommended some further studies, a CT scan. The CT revealed significant fractures about the face in almost every bone but the eye. Usually I would beat myself up because I had made the wrong diagnosis even though the right thing was done for the patient. I long for perfection and infinite wisdom in every aspect of my life. Today, however, I realize I learned a great deal from this patient. Hopefully, when I see similar injuries again I will have a better clue even before I recommend further studies.

What is different tonight is that I am learning a little about acceptance, especially about acceptance that I sometimes make the right decision for the wrong reasons. When I make the right choice for the wrong reason, is it possible that God may be guiding me in my ignorance? Is this an example of God doing for us what we can not do for ourselves?

I have had this experience so many times in my life. My earliest memory of it in my practice was almost forty years ago when I was an intern. I recommended surgery for a patient who had just recently had a heart attack because I thought he had acute gall bladder disease. The next morning I learned his gall bladder had been fine at surgery, but he needed the surgery because his appendix had ruptured.

Can I learn to rejoice when the right decision is made, learn from my mistakes and give thanks that somehow I may be directed onto the right path through no fault of my own? God may certainly be there guiding me also when I do make good choices by using my present knowledge.

However, I have a real tendency to believe that I made these "right" decisions because of my own knowledge that I have worked so hard to obtain on my own. I am not prone to give others (even God) credit when it is so obvious my own good works are shining through. I seem only to receive glimpses of the real truth about who is in charge when I am in contact with my own vulnerability.

My mind goes back to the computer screen. The laboratory results of our patient are posted. The tests are not good. Her surgeon comes in. We decide to go to her bedside and perform another ultrasound to look at the anatomy of this newly transplanted kidney.

The ultrasound shows very strong evidence that her kidney has lost the major part of its blood supply. It seems hopeless. Her surgeon, however, decides to give her a little more time before removing the kidney.

Early the next morning the ultrasound tech and I return to her bedside. This blond-haired little girl is asleep, and her mother sits in a chair beside her. We try to perform our test without waking the child.

As the ultrasound technologist directs the transducer to the transplanted kidney, we both look at each other in amazement. We are witnessing a real miracle: we hear and see the musical sounds of blood flow that has returned to that kidney. The kidney is alive!

There is very little in medical science to explain what has happened. I look at her mother and she looks back at our astonished faces and smiles. She, too, has some insight into the miracle we are seeing and hearing.

Healings, miracles take place daily that defy our good works and knowledge. I know that they don't just happen on Marshall Street where our hospital is located, but on Main Street, on Mississippi, on Broad. I know I am blind to most of the miracles that happen daily in my life, but somehow this week, I was given some new glasses.

Prayer for In the Evening

O Lord, support us all the day long, until the shadows lengthen, and the evening comes, and the busy world is hushed, and the fever of life is over, and our work is done. Then in thy mercy, grant us a safe lodging, and a holy rest, and peace at the last. Amen. —BCP, p. 833.

Good Samaritan

"But he, desiring to justify himself, said to Jesus, 'And who is my neighbor?'" Luke 10: 29-37.

I go to the hospital early in the morning to visit a member of our congregation who is having heart surgery. There is no one at the check-in desk. The clerk and the hospital volunteer are at another part of the waiting room talking intently about some issue. I wait for several minutes.

Finally the clerk says in a very annoyed voice, "If you are checking in for a procedure, just have a seat over there."

I respond, "I am trying to find someone who is having surgery this morning."

The volunteer looks at her list and responds, "You are in the wrong clinic and must go to another part of the hospital."

She takes me out into the hall and points to a place at some distance and tells me to go there and turn just by a linen cart to reach an elevator. I don't see any linen cart.

She says, "It is right there, just go on."

I walk down the hall and meet a dead end. It is getting late. I may miss seeing Sandra before her surgery.

Suddenly there appears an African American man pushing his housekeeping cart. I ask him, "Could you direct me to CVICU?"

He pushes his cart into a corner, leaves it, and responds, "Let me take you there."

We travel up two more floors, around a maze of corridors, and finally we arrive at CVICU.

"Thank you so much for bringing me here. I don't think I could have found this on my own."

His only response is, "This is my job."

And Jesus said, "Which of the three proved to be a good neighbor?"

Prayer for Health Care Providers

Sanctify, O Lord, those whom you have called to the study and practice of the arts of healing, and to the prevention of disease and pain. Strengthen them by your life-giving Spirit, that by their ministries the health of the community may be promoted and your creation glorified; through Jesus Christ our Lord. Amen. —*BCP*, p. 460.

Will Hallie Go Home?

"And ye now therefore have sorrow: but I will see you again, and your heart shall rejoice." John 16: 22.

In the mail was a large package. It was a handmade picture album from the mother of Hallie, a nine-month-old little girl who lived her entire life in our neonatal intensive care nursery. Hallie's mother had titled the album *Will Hallie Go Home.*

At Children's Hospital we daily see miracles, children who are miraculously brought back to life, restored to health. We daily see the blind see again, the deaf hear, the lame walk. But not everyone receives a miracle, and Hallie was one of these.

She died in her mother's arms in our intensive care unit one stormy Friday night when a tornado descended on our city. Many of the hospital staff went to Hallie's funeral over two hundred miles away in another state. One of her neonatologists wrote a poem about Hallie, "Weep Not," which her parents had engraved on her memorial stone. This same physician wrote:

> *Hallie's was not the first family that I became close to, nor the first family to share their faith with me, but I learned a tremendous amount by taking care of Hallie. I learned about the relationship between the subjective and the objective in the healing process, about the importance of families as surrogates for patients for whom*

consciousness is limited, about how the lives of complete strangers can become so closely intertwined.

The ministers in this story, as is often the case, are not ordained.

I learned about Hallie by not only reading her X-rays but also by playing the harp at her bedside at Christmas and shortly before she died. I learned from Hallie and her parents a faith and grief beyond words, a faith that knew that their daughter was still in God's good hands even if she had reluctantly slipped out of theirs.

It has been over a year since I received Hallie's picture album. Today a second item arrives in the mail, a note with these words from Hallie's mother in reply to my request to tell her story:

> *Hopefully Hallie's story will be of comfort to someone who is struggling with the lack of hope, the forever dagger that death pushes into our hearts as if to separate us from any peace. With all that Hallie taught us, I would certainly proclaim that one great thing she left us with is the renewal of hope. I know we will see her again. We never say we "lost" our daughter, because we know exactly where she is. And she is waiting for us there with Jesus. That hope keeps me and sustains me. Hallie's story is about a sick child who struggled, the parents who hurt so unbearably, the doctors and staff who worked to save the child they had come to love. The one thing I do hope you will keep in our story is the scripture from John that gives us the hope we stand upon: "And ye now therefore have sorrow: but I will see you again, and your heart shall rejoice."*

I set the letter down, walk to my bookshelf, and pull out *Will Hallie Go Home*. I sit on the couch and open the album, Hallie's mother's words and Hallie's presence encompassing me.

> *Hello. My name is Hallie Stewart and I wonder if I am ever going to get to go home. I have a heart and lung condition that has kept me in the hospital all my life. The doctors and nurses have taken*

such good care of me. I have heard sweet music here, and have dressed up, especially on holidays. My Mommy talks to me about home. She says it is a perfect place and that I will be completely happy. It sounds wonderful. Does God throw things when His heart is full of anguish for His children when their hearts are breaking? I think so. On a Friday evening in May, a tornado came to Little Rock causing much damage. It was then, while Mommy held me close, and Daddy held us both, that I went home.

"And behold it came to pass, as they still went on, and talked, that behold there appeared a chariot of fire and horses of fire, and parted them both asunder; and Elijah went up by a whirlwind into Heaven." 2 Kings 2:11.

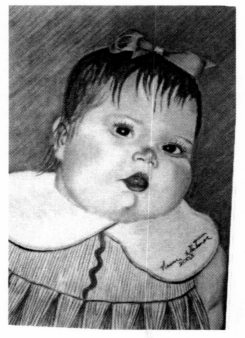

Hallie
(Drawing by Naomi Whitmer)
www.naomiart.com

Weep Not

Weep not,
  family, friend or stranger,
    for my moment on earth
      was but a preparation.

My heart beats on in the love you share;
  your joys are ever my smiles;
    your compassion is my strength;
      your hope, my very breath.

In your memories I sleep;
  in your creativity I run and play;
    in your flashes of insight
      I see the world anew.

Now I hold your hand when you are sad,
  kneel beside you as you pray,
    laugh with your amusement,
      and sing whenever you listen.

Weep not, then, for me;
  this body holds me back no longer;
    my spirit soars with yours,
      and our journey has just begun.

—Donnal Walter MD

Courtney

"A great windstorm arose, and the waves beat into the boat, so that the boat was already being swamped. But he was in the stern, asleep on the cushion; and they woke him up and said to him. 'Teacher, do you not care that we are perishing?' He woke up and rebuked the wind, and said to the sea, 'Peace! Be still!' Then the wind ceased, and there was a dead calm." Mark 5: 37- 39.

We knew Courtney before she was born. Bryant and Margaret were so excited about the birth of their first child. Courtney was an especially adorable baby girl. She could have been a model for a Renaissance cherub angel. Bryant being the proud new father in his pediatric residency examined his very attractive daughter at ten days using his new pediatric skills. To his surprise, her head was larger than it should be. Tests showed a lesion in her brain. Surgery to try to repair the abnormality left her extremely neurologically impaired.

Bryant and Margaret wanted to go on with their life. Courtney and our own daughter were baptized together on a sunny fall Sunday morning. We had a party at our home afterwards to honor both girls and all the friends of Margaret and Bryant who had supported them through this difficult time.

We kept in contact intermittently with Bryant and Margaret after they moved to Gulfport, Mississippi to practice pediatrics. The first home they bought was selected specifically because it was handicap accessible. Courtney lived at home for many years with her three younger brothers before she was hospitalized. I had heard through mutual friends that she had died when she was twenty-one years old.

* * *

Today I sit at the conference room at Trinity Cathedral at a deacon weekend meeting. One of our group, Emily, has just returned from Gulfport as part of a mission team after Hurricane Katrina has devastated the Gulf Coast. She talks about the destruction of homes, businesses, cities, and lives. Then she shows us pictures of the ruins of much of Gulfport.

It is too hard to comprehend. For some reason, I want to look at every picture as several albums are passed around. One set of pictures is from the Episcopal Church, St. Peter's By the Sea. The church is not recognizable. It is a complete loss. The next set of photographs show the devastated churchyard, devoid of tress and full of debris. I am greatly moved as I stare at the one thing standing in the churchyard, the graceful statue of an angel lifting her hands upward.

I ask Emily about the statue. She says the first day they were there it was on the ground. The next day they went back and a group from Tennessee had lifted it upright. She as well was moved by the statue and photographed it, and then something told her she should photograph the inscription beneath it.

Emily pulls out another picture showing the inscription on brass at the base. It is a memorial. I adjust my glasses and hold the picture up close. As I make out the writing, tears begin to stream down my cheeks.

Given in loving memory of Courtney Leigh McCrary,
June 14, 1979 – May 3, 2000,
by her godparents Rob and Stella McCrary.

I can think of nothing else for the rest of the meeting but Courtney's Angel.

In the midst of ruin and destruction I see this haunting angel lifting us out of the chaos. The statue is an icon reminding me that there is angel still standing there in the midst of the most horrendous sorrow and pain beside every patient I visit either for medical care or for a pastoral visit. I am reminded that the angel's presence is in the patient herself as well as in family members, friends, and those caring for the patient. Courtney and all the people in these stories have also taught me that our presence alone hopefully can also bring the message that there is something more than the surrounding disorder and confusion.

As I leave the meeting, Emily gives me the two pictures of Courtney's statue. I walk out the door into the Cathedral courtyard knowing that this tribute to Courtney and her life will be a constant sign in my life of God's presence in the midst of the most terrible suffering.

Dismissal

Let us go forth into the world, rejoicing in the power of the Spirit. Thanks be to God. Alleluia, alleluia. —*BCP*, p. 366.

Courtney's Angel in Churchyard of St. Peter's By the Sea,
Gulfport, Mississippi, After Hurricane Katrina

Acknowledgements

A grateful and heartfelt thank you to all of the families who lovingly offered their photos and memories.

Photograph of Courtney's Angel by Emily Bost. The artist who created the statue was a student at William Carey College. Records of his name were lost in Hurricane Katrina in 2005 when it devastated the Mississippi Gulf Coast.

Photograph of Dr. Seibert by Sean Moorman.
www.seanmoormanphoto.com

Scripture Readings from the *New Revised Standard Version* of the Bible and the *Revised Standard Version* of the Bible.

Book of Common Prayer (BCP), According to the use of The Episcopal Church. New York: Oxford University Press, 1979 Edition.

Enriching Our Worship 2: Ministry With the Sick and Dying. Supplemental Liturgical Material Prepared by the Standing Liturgical Commission. New York: Church Publishing Incorporated, 2000.

A New Zealand Prayer Book: The Anglican Church in Aotearoa, New Zealand and Polynesia. San Francisco: Harper, 1997.

The Union Prayerbook for Jewish Worship: Part II. New York: Central Conference of American Rabbis, 1958.

Walking the Mourner's Path, Transforming Grief into Joyful Living. Scottsdale,

AZ: Mourner's Path. www.mournerspath.com.

Book of Occasional Services. New York: Church Publishing, 2003.

"Weep Not" by Dr. Donnal Walter.

≈

The following stories have appeared previously:

"The Grandmother" in *The Living Church*, April 12, 1992. Copyright © 1992 by Joanna J. Seibert.

"Laura's Easter Corsage" appeared as "Easter Corsages" in *The Living Church*, April 7, 1996. Copyright © 1996 by Joanna J. Seibert.

"Magnificat" in *The Living Church*, December 17, 2000. Copyright © 2000 by Joanna J. Seibert.

"Teachers" appeared as "Wise Beyond His Years" in *The Living Church*, December 14, 2003. Copyright © 2003 by Joanna J. Seibert.

"Four Marys" appeared as "Mary at the Cross" in *The Living Church*, April 5, 1998. Copyright © 1998 by Joanna J. Seibert.

"First Day Back" appeared as "Abiding Effects" in *Sermons that Work XII, Preaching as Pastoral Caring*, Morehouse, 2005, edited by David Schlafer and Roger Alling. Copyright © 2005 by Joanna J. Seibert.

"Easter on Ash Wednesday" appeared as "Resurrection on Ash Wednesday" in *The Workbook of Episcopal Church Women of Arkansas*, March 1992. Copyright © 1992 by Joanna J. Seibert.

About the Author

Rev. Joanna J. Seibert, MD, is a pediatric radiologist at Arkansas Children's Hospital and the University of Arkansas Medical Sciences who has been an ordained deacon in the Diocese of Arkansas for five years. She is presently assigned to Trinity Episcopal Cathedral Little Rock. For eight years, she and her husband were Arkansas' representatives to the National Cathedral Association in Washington, DC.

Printed in the United States
71904LV00009B/49-84